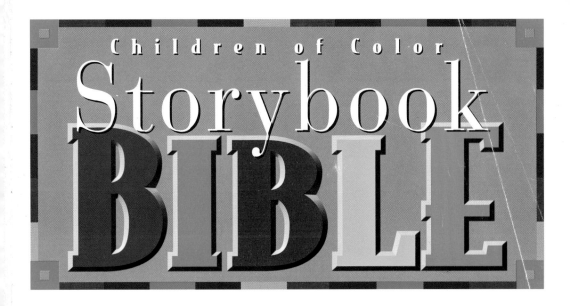

Children of Color
Storybook
BIBLE

with stories
from the
Contemporary English Version

children of
color

Atlanta

Thomas Nelson Publishers
Nashville

Contents

Stories from the Old Testament

Stories from the New Testament

Welcome to the Contemporary English Version

Languages are spoken before they are written. And far more communication is done through the spoken word than through the written word. In fact, more people hear the Bible read than read it for themselves. Traditional translations of the Bible count on the *reader's* ability to understand a *written* text. But the *Contemporary English Version* differs from all other English Bibles—past and present—in that it takes into consideration the needs of the *hearer*, as well as those of the reader, who may not be familiar with traditional biblical language.

The Contemporary English Version has been described as a "user-friendly" and a "mission-driven" translation that can be read aloud without stumbling, heard without misunderstanding, and listened to with enjoyment and appreciation, because the language is contemporary and the style is lucid and lyrical.

The *Contemporary English Version* invites you to *read*, to *hear*, to *understand* and to *share*

the Word of God now
as never before!

To Parents

> Love the LORD your God with all your heart, soul, and strength. Memorize his laws and tell them to your children over and over again. Talk about them all the time, whether you're at home or walking along the road or going to bed at night, or getting up in the morning.
>
> *Deuteronomy 6.5–7*

Using Children of Color Storybook Bible

This marvelous instruction from God's Word is a guideline for all parents in leading their children to the Lord. We are told to first *love* the Lord, then memorize his Word, his laws. Once we have our own relationship with God, he will lead us in talking about him and his Word to our children.

We hope this book will help. Its design is two-fold: 1) for parents to read to their younger children, sharing with them the marvelous adventures and lessons from the Bible; and 2) for older children to read for themselves, exploring the world of the Bible and the people who gave birth to our faith. The main text of the stories is from the Contemporary English Version, which is easy for children to understand, both as it is read to them and as they learn to read for themselves. Occasionally, some transitional paragraphs have been provided in order to move children from one story to another. These are printed in a slightly lighter typeface, so they can be distinguished from the actual Bible text, which is darker.

Most parents hope that their children will come to love the Lord. We can help by providing them with the stories they love and understand, explaining to them how much God loves each and every one of them, and, most importantly, by being a spiritual model for them.

A Word from Children of Color

Children of Color Publishing has chosen to develop Bible products that help to build the self-esteem of young people of African descent and has thoughtfully and prayerfully designed the *Children of Color Storybook Bible* for your child of color.

Young people need to understand that their heritage and history began long before civil rights and slavery and that the events and stories in the Bible are a part of that heritage—they took place on the very continent, Africa, especially northeastern Africa, where their ancestors lived and died. Knowing this can help children gain the confidence and courage to overcome the many obstacles they will encounter growing up in the world today.

Children are fearfully and wonderfully made. They should know that they are made in the image of God and that the Bible is talking about them when they read that believers can be victorious through Christ (Romans 8.37). They will profit greatly from being personally convinced that Christ can give them the strength to face anything (Philippians 3.14), and—most importantly—that Christ is their personal Savior. Presenting the Bible in a way to which African-American children and other minorities can relate makes achieving the goal much easier.

Give your children an early start: Read this beautiful Bible with your children daily. Teach them the principles that are in each story. Instill in them at an early age that the Bible is God's Word and our foundation for living. The best way to show your kids how to be a part of God's family, however, is to live your relationship with the Lord openly. Let them see you reading your own Bible and enjoying your own place in God's kingdom.

Children of Color
Storybook
BIBLE

The Story of Creation

In the beginning the earth was dark and empty. There was nothing to see—no people, no animals, and no trees. Not a living thing existed. God said, "I command light to shine!"

And light started shining. He separated light from darkness and named the light "Day" and the darkness "Night." That was the first day[a] that the LORD made.

On the second day God created the sky. That was the second day that the LORD made.

On the third day God said, "I command the water under the sky to come together in one place, so there will be dry ground." And that's what happened. God named the dry ground "Land," and he named the water "Ocean." He also commanded that the plants, trees, fruit, and grain grow. Beautiful greenery filled the earth. **God looked at what he had done and saw that it was good.** That was the third day that the LORD made.

On the fourth day **God said, "I command lights to appear in the sky and to separate day from night and to show the time for seasons, special days, and years.** God also made two powerful lights, the brighter one, called the sun, to rule the day

and the other, called the moon, to rule the night. Then God made the stars and put them and the rest of the lights in the sky to shine on the earth. **God looked at what he had done, and it was good.** That was the fourth day that the LORD made.

On the fifth day God created the living creatures of the sea and birds to fly above the earth. **Then he gave the living creatures his blessing—he told the ocean creatures to live everywhere in the ocean and the birds to live everywhere on earth.** That was the fifth day that the LORD made.

On the sixth day God created all kinds of tame and wild animals. This was the day he also created the people to be like himself. They would rule the fish, birds, and other living creatures. **God looked at what he had done.** All of it was very good! That was the sixth day that the LORD made.

By the seventh day God had finished his work, and so he rested. God blessed the seventh day and made it special. God was very pleased with all he had done.

from Genesis 1.1—2.3

the first day: A day was measured from evening to evening.

Adam and Eve

The Lord God took a handful of soil and made a man[a]. God breathed life into the man, and the man started breathing. The first man was called Adam. The Lord made a garden in a place called Eden. The Lord God put the man in the Garden of Eden to take care of it and to look after it. The Garden of Eden was a beautiful place. The Lord God placed all kinds

of beautiful trees and fruit trees in the garden. Two other trees were in the middle of the garden. One of the trees gave life—the other gave the power to know the difference between right and wrong.

God told Adam, "You may eat fruit from any tree in the garden, except the one that has the power to let you know the difference between right and wrong. If you eat any fruit from that tree, you will die before the day is over!"

God decided it was not good for man to live alone. God

put Adam in a deep sleep and removed one of his ribs. The LORD made a woman out of the rib. Her name was Eve. Eve was the first woman. When Adam woke up, he was excited to see another person.

Adam and Eve lived happily in the Garden of Eden obeying God's rules and enjoying the beautiful plants and animals.

Now the snake was sneakier than any of the other wild animals that the LORD God had made. One day it came to the woman and asked, "Did God tell you not to eat fruit from any tree in the garden?"

The woman answered, "God said we could eat fruit from any tree in the garden, except the one in the middle. He told us not to eat fruit from that tree or even to touch it. If we do, we will die."

"No, you won't!" the snake replied. "God understands what will happen on the day you eat from that tree. You will see what you have done, and you will know the difference between right and wrong, just as God does."

Eve wanted the wisdom that the tree would give her. So she took a piece of fruit from the tree and bit it! Her husband was there with her, so she gave some to him, and he ate it too. Right away they saw what they had done, and they realized they had disobeyed God. They became frightened and tried to hide from God.

Later, the LORD called out to Adam. "Where are you? Why are you hiding yourself from me? Did you eat any fruit from that tree in the middle of the garden?"

Adam answered, "It was the woman you put here with me. She gave me some of the fruit, and I ate it."

God asked Eve, "What have you done?"

"The snake tricked me," she answered. "And I ate some of that fruit." So the LORD cursed the snake to crawl on his stomach and eat dirt. Then He cursed Eve to suffer terribly during childbirth.

To Adam the LORD said, "You listened to your wife and ate fruit from that tree.

> And so, the ground will be under a curse because of what you did. As long as you live, you will have to struggle to grow enough food. Your food will be plants, but the ground will produce thorns and thistles. You will have to sweat to earn a living; you were made out of soil, and you will once again turn into soil."

So the LORD God sent them out of the Garden of Eden, where they would have to work the ground from which the man had been made.

***from* Genesis 2.7—3.23**

ᵃ*man:* In Hebrew "man" comes from the same word as "soil."

Cain
and Abel

After being thrown out of the Garden of Eden, Adam and Eve had two sons. Their names were Cain and Abel. Abel became a sheep farmer, but Cain farmed the land.

One day, Cain gave part of his harvest to the LORD,

and Abel also gave an offering to the LORD. He unselfishly gave the LORD his first-born lamb. The LORD was pleased with Abel and his offering, but not with Cain and his offering. This made Cain so angry that he could not hide his feelings.

The LORD said to Cain:

What's wrong with you? Why do you have such an angry look on your face? If you had done the right thing, you would be smiling.^a But you did the wrong thing, and now sin is waiting to attack you like a lion. Sin wants to destroy you, but don't let it!

Cain said to his brother Abel, "Let's go for a walk."[b] And when they were out in a field, Cain killed him.

Afterwards the LORD asked Cain, "Where is Abel?"

"How should I know?" he answered. "Am I supposed to look after my brother?"

Then the LORD said:

Why have you done this terrible thing? You killed your own brother, and his blood flowed onto the ground. Now his blood is calling out for me to punish you. And so, I'll put you under a curse. Because you killed Abel and made his blood run out on the ground, you will never be able to farm the land again. If you try to farm the land, it won't produce anything for you. From now on, you'll be without a home, and you'll spend the rest of your life wandering from place to place.

"This punishment is too hard!" Cain said. "You're making me leave home and live far from you.[c] I will have to wander about without a home, and just anyone could kill me."

"No!"[d] the LORD answered. "Anyone who kills you will be punished seven times worse than I am punishing you." So the LORD put a mark on Cain to warn everyone not to kill him. But Cain had to go far from the LORD and live in the Land of Wandering,[e] which is east of Eden.

Genesis 4.2–16

[a]*you would be smiling:* Or "I would have accepted your offering." [b]*Cain said to his brother Abel, "Let's . . . walk":* Most ancient translations: Hebrew "Cain spoke to his brother Abel." [c]*live . . . you:* At this time it was believed that the LORD was with his people only in their own land. [d]*No:* The ancient translations: Hebrew "Very well!" [e]*Wandering:* The Hebrew text has "Nod," which means "wandering."

Noah

There were many evil people on the earth, and God was not pleased with them. He said, "I'll destroy every living creature on earth! I'll wipe out people, animals, birds, and reptiles. I'm sorry I ever made them."

However, there was one man that pleased God. His name was Noah. Noah was the only person who lived right

and obeyed God. God told Noah that he was planning to destroy the whole world and all of its people. He instructed Noah to build a boat that was three stories high and put a door on one side. He promised Noah that he, his wife, his sons, and their wives would be kept safe in the boat, or ark as this boat is sometimes called.

The LORD told Noah:

Take your whole family with you into the boat, because you are the only one on this earth who pleases me.

Take two of every animal. One male and one female. Do this so there will always be animals and birds on the earth. Seven days from now I will send rain that will last forty days and nights, and I will destroy all other living creatures I have made.

Noah did exactly as God told him. Noah, his family, and the animals got in the ark just as God said.

For forty days the rain poured down without stopping. Water even came up out of the earth. The water became deeper and deeper, until the boat started floating high above the ground. Finally, the mighty flood was so deep that even the highest mountain peaks were covered by the water. Not a bird, animal, reptile, or human was left alive anywhere on earth. The LORD destroyed everything that breathed. Nothing was left alive except Noah and the others in the boat. They had trusted and obeyed God.

God was again pleased. He blessed Noah and his family for their obedience. God promised never to destroy the earth with a flood again. God placed a rainbow of magnificent colors in the sky as a sign of his promise.

God said to Noah and his sons:

The rainbow that I have put in the sky will be my sign to you and to every living creature on earth. It will remind you that I will keep this promise forever. When I send clouds over the earth, and a rainbow appears in the sky, I will remember my promise to you and to all other living creatures. Never again will I let floodwaters destroy all life. When I see the rainbow in the sky, I will always remember the promise I have made to every living creature. The rainbow will be a sign of that solemn promise.

from **Genesis 6.5—9.17**

Nimrod and the Descendants of Ham

After the flood, Noah and his sons, Shem, Ham, and Japheth, came out of the boat. Ham later had a son named Canaan. All people on earth are descendants of Noah's three sons. Ham was the father of Ethiopia,[a] Egypt, Put, and

Canaan, and they were the ancestors of the kingdoms named after them.

Ham's descendants had their own languages, tribes, and land. They were Ethiopia, Egypt, Put, and Canaan. African-American people and other people of color, such as Asians and Indians, are descendants of Ham.

One of Ham's descendants, Cush, was the father of many sons, and he was also the ancestor of Nimrod, a mighty warrior whose strength came from the LORD. Nimrod is the reason for the saying, "You hunt like Nimrod with the strength of the LORD!" Cush first ruled in Babylon, Erech, and Accad, all of which were in Babylonia. From there Nimrod went to Assyria and built the great city of Nineveh.

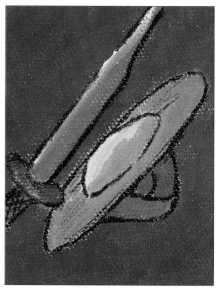

Nimrod was the world's first mighty warrior, and he also built many great cities. He also built Rehoboth-Ir and Calah, as well as Resen, which is between Nineveh and Calah. "Rehoboth-Ir" was Hebrew for "broad places of the city" and may have been a suburb of Nineveh. Calah was located between two great rivers. Later, it was the military headquarters of the Assyrians, and they launched some of their greatest battles from there. "Resen" means "fountainhead" and was part of a cluster of cities that was more than 60 miles across!

Nimrod was a great warrior and mighty hunter, but he was also a terrific king! Nimrod built a great kingdom in Assyria, which became known as "the land of Nimrod."

He also built an empire in the land of Shinar. Nimrod built the great city of Babel, which is where all the languages in the world came from. His other cities included Erech, Calneh, and Accad, which was the capital of an empire that ruled the Middle East for almost 300 years! In fact, Nimrod brought to the Middle East a new type of government that improved the way people lived, worked, and spent their money.

His reign over his kingdoms was so successful that many of the empires that ruled part of the Middle East for more than 2,000 years could be traced to the mighty warrior, Nimrod.

Genesis 9.19; 10.6–9

[a]*Ethiopia:* The Hebrew text has "Cush," which was a region south of Egypt that included parts of the present countries of Ethiopia and Sudan.

Sodom and Gomorrah

The LORD said, "Abraham, I have heard that the people of Sodom and Gomorrah are doing all kinds of evil things. Now I am going down to see for myself if those people really are that bad. If they aren't, I want to know about it."

Abraham asked, "Lᴏʀᴅ, when you destroy the evil people, are you also going to destroy those who are good? Wouldn't you spare the city if there are only fifty good people in it? You surely wouldn't let them be killed when you destroy the evil ones. You are the judge of all the earth, and you do what is right."

The Lᴏʀᴅ replied, "If I find fifty good people in Sodom, I will save the city to keep them from being killed."

Abraham answered, "I am nothing more than the   23

dust of the earth. Please forgive me, LORD, for daring to speak to you like this. But suppose there are only forty-five good people in Sodom. Would you still wipe out the whole city?"

"If I find forty-five good people," the LORD replied, "I won't destroy the city."

"Suppose there are just forty good people?" Abraham asked.

"Even for them," the LORD replied, "I won't destroy the city."

Abraham said, "Please don't be angry, LORD, if I ask you what you will do if there are only thirty good people in the city?"

"If I find thirty," the LORD replied, "I still won't destroy it."

Then Abraham said, "I don't have any right to ask you, LORD, but what would you do if you find only twenty?"

"Because of them, I won't destroy the city," was the LORD's answer.

Finally, Abraham said, "Please don't get angry, LORD, if I speak just once more. Suppose you find only ten good people there?"

"For the sake of ten good people," the LORD told him, "I still won't destroy the city."

Lot was the nephew of Abraham, and he lived in Sodom with his family. Lot was one of the very few "good people" who lived in Sodom. Two angels appeared to Lot and told him to leave Sodom with his family and not to look back at the destruction of the city.

After Lot and his family ran from the city, the LORD sent burning sulfur down like rain on Sodom and Gomorrah. He destroyed those cities and everyone who lived in them.

In disobedience, Lot's wife stopped to look back at the burning cities. Instantly, she was turned into a block of salt. But the LORD remembered his promise to Abraham and saved Lot from the terrible destruction.

Genesis 18.20−19.29

Abraham and Isaac

Abraham and Sarah were very old, and Sarah was well past the age for having children. Even so, the LORD promised that they would have a son, and the LORD did bless them with a fine son. His name was Isaac.

Some years later God decided to test Abraham. The LORD said, "Go get Isaac, your only son, the one you dearly love! Take him to the land of Moriah, and I will show you a mountain where you must sacrifice him to me on the fires of an altar."

So Abraham got up early the next morning and chopped wood for the fire. Abraham, Isaac, a donkey, and two servants set out for the place where God had instructed him to go.

Three days later Abraham looked off in the distance and saw the place. He told his servants, "Stay with the donkey, while my son and I go over there to worship. We will come back."

Abraham put the wood on Isaac's shoulder, but he carried the hot coals and the knife. As the two of them walked along, Isaac said, "Father, we have the coals and the wood, but where is the lamb for the sacrifice?"

"My son," Abraham answered, "God will provide the lamb."

The two reached the place where the LORD had told Abraham to go. Abraham built an altar and placed the wood on it. Next, he tied up his son and put him on the wood. He took the knife and got ready to kill his son. But the LORD's angel shouted from heaven, "Abraham! Abraham!"

"Here I am!" he answered.

"Don't hurt the boy or harm him in any way!" the angel said. "Now I know that you truly obey God, because you were willing to offer him your only son."

Abraham looked up and saw a ram caught by its horns in the bushes. So he took the ram and sacrificed it in the place of his son.

Abraham named that place "The LORD Will Provide."

And even now people say, "On the mountain of the LORD it will be provided."

The LORD's angel called out from heaven a second time:
You were willing to offer the LORD your only son, and so he makes you this solemn promise, "I will bless you and give you such a large family, that someday your descendants will be more numerous than the stars in the sky or the grains of sand along the beach. They will defeat their enemies and take over the cities where their enemies live. You have obeyed me, and so you and your descendants will be a blessing to all nations on the earth."

Abraham and Isaac went back to the servants who had come with him, and they returned to Abraham's home in Beersheba.

Genesis 22.1-19

The Birth of Moses

Most of the people of Israel lived in Egypt, and there were a lot of them. A new king came to power, and he did not like the Israelites. He said:

There are too many of those Israelites in our country, and they are becoming more powerful than we are.

The Israelites were forced to work harder in order to wear them down. But even though the Israelites were mistreated, their families grew larger, and they took over more land. Because of this, the Egyptians hated them worse than before and made them work so hard their lives were miserable.

Finally, the king called in Shiphrah and Puah, the two women who helped the Hebrew mothers when they gave birth. He told them, "If a Hebrew woman gives

31

birth to a girl, let the child live. If the baby is a boy, kill him!"

But the two women were faithful to God and did not kill the boys, even though the king had told them to. The king called them in again and asked, "Why are you letting those baby boys live?"

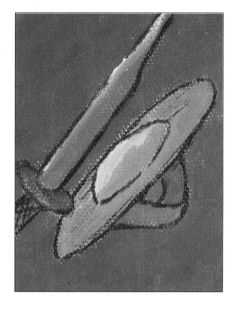

They answered, "Hebrew women have their babies much quicker than Egyptian women. By the time we arrive, their babies are already born. God was good to the two women because they truly respected him, and he blessed them with children of their own.

The Hebrews kept increasing until finally, the king gave a command to everyone in the nation. "As soon as a Hebrew boy is born, throw him into the Nile River! But you can let the girls live."

A married Israelite man and woman had a beautiful baby boy. Unable to keep him hidden after three months, the mother, Jochebed, made a basket, put the baby inside the basket, and placed it in the tall grass along the edge of the Nile River. The baby's older sister, Miriam, stood off at a distance to see what would happen to him.

At about this time one of the king's daughters came down with her women to bathe at the river. She saw the basket in the tall grass and sent one of the young women to pull it out of the water. When the king's daughter opened the basket, she saw the baby and felt sorry for him because he was crying. She said, "This must be one of the Hebrew babies."

At once, Miriam came up and asked, "Do you want me to get a Hebrew woman to take care of the baby for you?"

"Yes," the king's daughter answered.

So Miriam brought the baby's mother, Jochebed, to the king's daughter.

The baby's mother carried him home and took care of him. And when he was old enough, she took him to the king's daughter, who adopted him. She named him Moses, because the name Moses means "pulled from the water."

Exodus 1.6–10, 15–22; 2.1–10

Moses and Zipporah

Because the daughter of the Egyptian king had saved him, Moses lived with the Egyptians as he was growing up. He dressed and acted like an Egyptian, but he was still a Hebrew.

After he had grown up, he went out to where his own

people were hard at work, and he saw an Egyptian beating one of them. Moses looked around to see if anyone was watching, then he killed the Egyptian and hid his body in the sand.

When Moses went out the next day, he saw two Hebrews fighting. So he went to the man who had started the fight and asked, "Why are you beating up one of your own people?"

The man answered, "Who put you in charge of us and

35

made you our judge? Are you planning to kill me, just as you killed that Egyptian?"

This frightened Moses because he was sure that people must have found out what had happened. When the king

heard what Moses had done, the king wanted to kill him. But Moses escaped and went to the land of Midian. Many of the people of Midian, who were descendants of Noah's son Ham, were shepherds.

One day, Moses was sitting there by a well, when the seven daughters of Jethro, the priest of Midian,[a] came up to water their father's sheep and goats. Some shepherds tried to chase them away, but Moses came to their rescue and watered their animals. When Jethro's daughters returned home, their father asked, "Why have you come back so early today?"

They answered, "An Egyptian rescued us from the shepherds, and he even watered our sheep and goats."

"Where is he?" Jethro asked. "Why did you leave him out there? Invite him to eat with us."

Moses agreed to stay on with Jethro, who later let his daughter Zipporah marry Moses. And when she had a son, Moses said, "I will name him Gershom,[b] since I am a foreigner in this country." The name Gershom means "foreigner."

Now in those times, it was the law of God that all boys

must be circumcised before they were eight days old. This meant cutting a small flap of their skin, which meant that they worshiped the LORD God. To not circumcise your baby boy meant you were denying that you belonged to God.

Because Moses was unable to circumcise their son, Zipporah worried that the LORD would kill Moses. But Zipporah[c] circumcised her son with a flint knife. She touched his[d] legs with the skin she had cut off and said, "My dear son, this blood will protect you."[e] What she meant was that because she had circumcised the boy, she had done what God had ordered Moses to do. Now both her son and her husband would no longer be out of God's favor. Zipporah said to Moses, "Yes, my dear, you are safe because of this circumcision."[f]

from **Exodus 2.11–23; 4.24–26**

[a]*Jethro, the priest of Midian:* Hebrew "the priest of Midian." But his name is given in other verses. In the Hebrew of verse 18 he is spoken of as "Reuel," which may have been the name of the tribe to which Jethro belonged. [b]*Gershom:* In Hebrew "Gershom" sounds like "foreigner." [c]*Zipporah:* The wife of Moses. [d]*his:* Either Moses or the boy. [e]*My dear son . . . you:* Or "My dear husband, you are a man of blood" (meaning Moses). [f]*you are . . . circumcision:* Or "you are a man of blood."

The Exodus

The Israelites complained because they were forced to be slaves. They cried out to the LORD for help, and God heard their loud cries. He did not forget the promise he had made to Abraham, Isaac, and Jacob about the Israelite people.

The LORD decided to send Moses to free his people from Egypt. The LORD appeared to Moses in a burning bush. God said to Moses:

I have seen how my people are suffering as slaves in Egypt, and I have heard them beg for my help because of the way they are being mistreated. I feel sorry for them, and I have come down to rescue them from the Egyptians.

I will bring my people out of Egypt into a country where there is good land, rich with milk and honey. Now go to the king! I am sending you to lead my people out of this country.

But Moses said, "Who am I to go to the king and lead your people out of Egypt?"

God replied, "I will be with you. And you will know that I am the one who sent you."

Moses, along with his brother Aaron, did as the LORD commanded and went to Egypt. Unfortunately, the king refused to let the Israelite slaves go. He was a very stubborn king. Only after God sent ten different types of troubles on him and his people did the king finally decide to let the Israelites go.

"Get your people out of my country and leave us alone! Go and worship the LORD, as you have asked. Take your sheep, goats, and cattle, and get out."

The Israelites, led by Moses, walked out of Egypt and began their journey through the desert to the land the LORD had promised.

When the king of Egypt heard that the Israelites had finally left, he and his officials changed their minds. They realized they no longer had their obedient slaves to work for them.

The king got his war chariot and army ready. They were going after Moses and the Israelite caravan to return them to Egypt.

The Israelites were camping by the Red Sea. When they saw the king coming with his army of at least six hundred chariots, they were frightened and begged for the LORD to help. They also complained to Moses, "Wasn't there enough room in Egypt to bury us? Is that why you brought us out here to die in the desert? Why did you bring us out of Egypt anyway? While we were there, didn't we tell you to leave us alone? We had rather be slaves in Egypt than die in this desert!"

But Moses answered, "Don't be afraid? Be brave, and you will see the Lord save you today. These Egyptians will never bother you again. The Lord will fight for you, and you won't have to do a thing."

The Lord said to Moses, "Tell the Israelites to move forward. Then hold your walking stick over the sea. The water will open up and make a road where they can walk through on dry ground. I will make the Egyptians so stubborn that they will go after you. Then I will be praised because of what happens to the king and his chariots and calvary."

A large cloud moved between the Egyptians and the Israelites. The cloud gave light for the Israelites and darkness for the Egyptians.

Moses stretched his arm over the sea, and the Lord sent a strong east wind that blew all night until there was dry land where the water had been. The sea opened up, and the Israelites walked through on dry land with a wall of water on each side.

The Egyptian chariots and calvary went after them. When all the Israelites made it to the other side, the Lord instructed Moses to again stretch his arms across the sea. The walls of water came down and covered the Egyptians. Not one soldier remained alive.

On that day the Israelites knew that the Lord had saved them, and they worshiped the Lord and trusted his servant Moses.

Jethro

Jethro was a descendant of Ham, and he was a kind, just, and wise Midianite priest. He was the father of Moses' wife, Zipporah. Moses and Zipporah had met while she was watching her father's sheep; so Jethro was a shepherd as well as a good priest for God.

Jethro understood how important it is to do the

things that God asks us to do. When he saw that his son-in-law, Moses, had been called to greatness on behalf of the LORD, Jethro did everything he could to help Moses fulfill his purpose. And he heard what the LORD God had done for Moses and his people, after rescuing them from Egypt.

In the meantime, Moses had sent his wife Zipporah and her two sons to stay with Jethro, who watched over them during the time when Moses was leading the Israelites out of Egypt. While Moses and the people of Israel were camped

43

near Mount Sinai[a] Jethro sent Moses this message: "I am coming to visit you, and I am bringing your wife and two sons."

When they arrived, Moses went out and bowed down in front of Jethro, then kissed him. After they had greeted each other, they went into the tent, where Moses told him everything the LORD had done to protect Israel against the Egyptians and their king. He also told him how the LORD had helped them in all of their troubles.

Jethro was so pleased to hear this good news about what the LORD had done, that he shouted, "Praise the LORD! He rescued you and the Israelites from the Egyptians and their king. Now I know that the LORD is the greatest God, because he has rescued Israel from their arrogant enemies."

The next morning Moses sat down at the place where he decided legal cases for the people, and everyone crowded around him until evening. Jethro saw how much Moses had to do for the people, and he asked, "Why are you the only judge? Why do you let these people crowd around you from morning till evening?"

Moses answered, "Because they come here to find out what God wants them to do. They bring their complaints to me, and I make decisions on the basis of God's laws."

Jethro replied:

That isn't the best way to do it. You and the people who come to you will soon be worn out. The job is too much for one person; you can't do it alone. God will help you if you follow my advice. You should be the one to speak to God for the people, and you should teach them God's laws and show them what they must do to live right.

You will need to choose some leaders who love God and are honest. These judges can handle the ordinary cases and bring the more difficult ones to you.

Moses followed Jethro's advice and appointed other leaders to help him. Then Jethro, the wise advisor and priest, returned home.

Exodus 18.1–22, 24, 25, 27

ªMount Sinai: Hebrew "the mountain of God."   *45*

The Ten Commandments

Moses led the Israelites out of Egypt. After traveling for two months, they set up camp in the desert at the foot of Mount Sinai.

Moses went up the mountain to meet with the LORD God, who told him to say to the people:

You saw what I did in Egypt, and you know how I

brought you here to me, just as a mighty eagle carries its young. Now if you will faithfully obey me, you will be my very own people. The world is mine, but you will be my holy nation and serve me as priests.

Moses went back down the mountain and told the people what God had said and they promised to do everything the LORD commanded. The people gathered at the foot of the mountain to hear God's words. Smoke poured out of the mountain just like a furnace, and the whole mountain shook. Moses spoke, and God answered him with thunder. God said to the people of Israel:

I am the LORD your God, the one who brought you out of Egypt where you were slaves.

1. Do not worship any god except me.

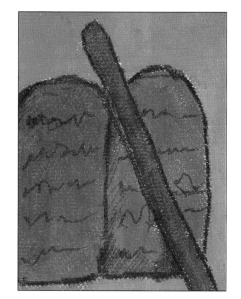

2. Do not make idols that look like anything in the sky or on earth or in the ocean under the earth. Don't bow down and worship idols.

3. Do not misuse my name.[a]

4. Remember that the Sabbath Day belongs to me. You have six days when you can do your work, but the seventh day of each week belongs to me, your God. No one is to work on that day.

5. Respect your father and your mother.

6. Do not murder.

7. Be faithful in marriage.

8. Do not steal.

9. Do not tell lies about others.

10. Do not want anything that belongs to someone else.

The people trembled with fear when they heard the thunder and saw the lightning and the smoke coming from the mountain. They stood a long way off and said to Moses,

"If you speak to us, we will listen. But don't let God speak to us, or we will die!"

"Don't be afraid!" Moses replied. "God has come only to test you, so that by obeying him you won't sin." He explained how important it was that the people obey God. But when Moses went near the thick cloud where God was, the people stayed a long way off.

The LORD told Moses to say to the people of Israel:

> With your own eyes, you saw me speak to you from heaven. So you must never make idols of silver or gold to worship in place of me.[b]

Exodus 19.1–6, 14, 17–19; 20.1–23

^a*misuse my name:* Probably includes breaking promises, telling lies after swearing to tell the truth, using the LORD's name as a curse word or a magic formula, and trying to control the LORD by using his name. ^b*in place of me:* Or "together with me."

Joshua and the Walls of Jericho

Joshua was chosen by God to lead Israel across the Jordan River and into the land that God had promised them. God told Joshua, "Be strong and brave! Be careful to do everything my servant Moses taught you. Don't ever be afraid or

discouraged! I am the LORD your God, and I will be there to help you wherever you go."

One day, Joshua was near Jericho when he saw a man standing some distance in front of him. The man was holding a sword, so Joshua walked up to him and asked, "Are you on our side or on our enemies' side?"

"Neither," he answered. "I am here because I am the commander of the LORD's army."

Joshua fell to his knees and bowed down to the ground. "I am your servant," he said. "Tell me what to do."

"Take off your sandals," the commander answered. "This is a holy place."

So Joshua took off his sandals.

The people of Jericho had been locking the gates in their town wall because they were afraid of the Israelites. No one could go out or come in.

The LORD said to Joshua:

With my help, you and your army will defeat the king of Jericho and his army, and you will capture the town. Here is how to do it. March slowly around Jericho once a day for six days. Take along the sacred chest and have seven priests walk in front of it, carrying trumpets.[a]

But on the seventh day, march slowly around the town seven times while the priests blow their trumpets. Then the priests will blast on their trumpets, and everyone else will shout. The wall will fall down, and your soldiers can go straight in from every side.

Joshua and the Israelites did as the LORD commanded. And, on the seventh day the priests blew their trumpets again, and the soldiers shouted as loud as they could. The walls of Jericho fell flat. Then the soldiers rushed up the hill, went straight into the town, and captured it. They killed everyone in Jericho, even the animals.

The Israelites took the silver and gold and the things made of bronze and iron and put them with the rest of the treasure that was kept at the LORD's house. Finally, they set fire to Jericho and everything in it.

The LORD helped Joshua in everything he did because Joshua was loyal and faithful.

Joshua 1.6–9; 5.13–15; 6.1–27

Gideon

There was peace in Israel for about forty years. Then once again the Israelites started disobeying the LORD, so he let the nation of Midian control Israel for seven years. The Midianites were so cruel that many Israelites ran to the mountains and hid in caves.

Every time the Israelites would plant crops, the Midian-

ites invaded Israel. They rode in on their camels, set up their tents, and then let their livestock eat the crops. The Midianites stole food, sheep, cattle, and donkeys. Like a swarm of locusts, they could not be counted, and they ruined the land wherever they went.

One day an angel of the LORD appeared to Gideon, an Israelite, and said, "The LORD is helping you, and you are a strong warrior."

Gideon answered, "If the LORD is helping us, then why

55

have all these awful things happened? The LORD has abandoned us to the Midianites."

Then the LORD himself said, "Gideon, you will be strong, because I am giving you the power to rescue Israel from the Midianites."

Gideon replied, "But how can I rescue Israel? My clan is the weakest one in Manasseh, and everyone else in my family is more important than I am."

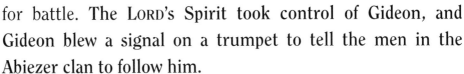

The LORD answered, "Defeating the Midianites will be as easy as beating up one man."

Gideon was finally ready for battle. The LORD's Spirit took control of Gideon, and Gideon blew a signal on a trumpet to tell the men in the Abiezer clan to follow him.

Gideon prayed to God, "I know that you promised to help me rescue Israel, but I need proof. Tonight I'll put some wool on the stone floor of that threshing place over there. If you really will help me rescue Israel, then tomorrow morning let there be dew on the wool, but let the stone floor be dry."

And that's just what happened.

The LORD said, "Gideon, your army is too big. I can't let you win with this many soldiers. The Israelites would think that they had won the battle all by themselves and that I didn't have anything to do with it." So Gideon's troops were cut from 35,000 men to only 10,000 men.

"Gideon," the LORD said, "you still have too many soldiers." So Gideon's troops were cut to just 300 men.

Gideon and his soldiers blew their trumpets, shouting "Fight for the LORD" and the LORD made the enemy soldiers pull out their swords and start fighting each other. The enemy army tried to escape from the camp, but the Israelites chased them, and eventually the army was destroyed.

The LORD created a plan for Gideon that would let him successfully conquer the Midianites. Gideon did just as the LORD told him, and the Midianites were defeated.

from Judges 6.16—7.21

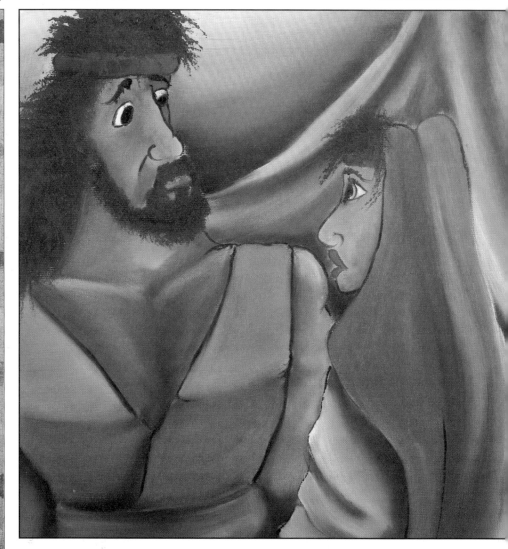

Samson
and Delilah

S amson was a strong and powerful man. As a young boy he had been blessed by the LORD with extraordinary strength. Once he tore a lion apart with his bare hands!

The Philistines hated Samson because he had used his

strength to kill many of them. They wanted to take their re-

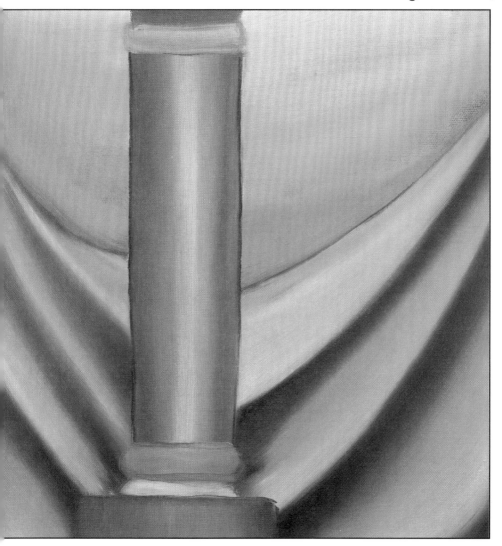

venge, but first they needed to find the secret to his enormous strength. What made Samson so powerful?

Some time later, Samson fell in love with a woman named Delilah who lived in Sorek Valley. The Philistine rulers went to Delilah and offered her money to find out the secret to Samson's strength.

The next time Samson was at Delilah's house, she asked, "Samson, what makes you so strong? How can I tie you up so you can't get away? Come on, you can tell me."

Samson answered, "If someone ties me up with seven new bowstrings that have never been dried,[a] it will make me just as weak as anyone else."

This was not true, and when Delilah tied him up, Samson snapped the bowstrings, as though they were pieces of scorched string. Delilah was angry, and begged Samson to tell her his secret. Because he didn't want to tell his secret, Samson fooled Delilah again and again, never revealing the secret of his strength. But Delilah nagged and pestered until Samson could stand it no longer.

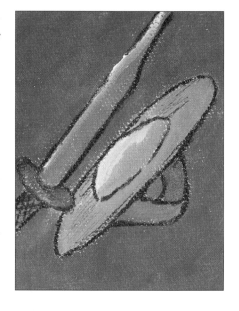

Finally, Samson told her the truth. "I have belonged to God[b] ever since I was born, so my hair has never been cut. If it were ever cut off, my strength would leave me, and I would be as weak as anyone else."

Delilah realized that he was telling the truth. So she sent someone to tell the Philistine rulers. Then she invited Samson back to her house.

With Samson asleep on her lap, she began cutting his hair. When she finished, she tied him up and shouted, "Samson, the Philistines are attacking!" Samson woke up and thought, "I'll break loose and escape, just as I always do." He did not realize that the LORD had stopped helping him.

The Philistines grabbed Samson and poked out his eyes. They took him to the prison in Gaza and chained him up. Then they put him to work, turning a millstone to grind grain. But they didn't cut his hair any more, so it started growing back.

One night the Philistine rulers threw a big party. They were celebrating in a temple packed with three thousand or more people. The rulers brought Samson out of prison, and everyone began making fun of him.

Samson prayed, "Please remember me, LORD God. The Philistines poked out my eyes, but make me strong one last time."

Samson was standing between the two middle columns that held up the roof. Then he shouted, "Let me die with the Philistines." He pushed against the columns as hard as he could and the temple collapsed with the Philistine rulers and everyone else still inside. Samson killed more Philistines when he died than he had killed during his entire life.

Judges 16.4–25, 27–30

^a*new bowstrings . . . dried:* The strings for a bow were often made from sinews or internal organs of animals. These strings were made while the animal tissues were still moist, and they became much stronger, once they were dry.
^b*belonged to God:* The Hebrew text has "be a Nazirite of God." Nazirites were dedicated to God and had to follow special rules to stay that way.

Ruth and Naomi

Before Israel was ruled by kings, Elimelech from the tribe of Eprath lived in the town of Bethlehem. His wife was named Naomi, and their two sons were Mahlon and Chilion. But when their crops failed, they moved to the country of Moab.[a] And while they were there, Elimelech died, leaving Naomi with only her two sons.

Later, Naomi's sons married Moab women. One was named Orpah and the other Ruth. About ten years later, Mahlon and Chilion also died. Now Naomi had no husband or sons.

When Naomi heard that the LORD had given his people a good harvest, she and her two daughters-in-law got ready to leave Moab and go to Judah. As they were on their way there, Naomi said to them, "Don't you want to go back home to your own mothers? You were kind to my husband and sons and you have always been kind to me. I pray that the LORD will be just as kind to you. May he give each of you another husband and a home of your own."

Naomi kissed them. The daughters-in-law still wanted

to go with Naomi. They loved her very much. Naomi tried to explain that it was best that they return to their own families. "Life is harder for me than it is for you, because the LORD has turned against me,"[b] Naomi told them. She believed the women had a better chance at a new life without her.

The women cried, but finally Orpah kissed her mother-in-law good-by. Ruth did not. She again pleaded with Naomi. Ruth told Naomi that she'd follow Naomi wherever she would go. She vowed to be by Naomi's side forever. When Naomi saw that Ruth had made up her mind to go with her, she stopped urging her to go back.

They reached Bethlehem, and the whole town was excited to see them.

Ruth went out to find work, and she found a job picking up grain in a field owned by a man named Boaz. He was a relative of Naomi's husband Elimelech, as well as a rich and important man. Boaz had heard how Ruth helped her mother-in-law, so he made Ruth's work easier. He also made sure that no one would treat or speak harshly to

Ruth.

Ruth worked in the fields until the barley and wheat were harvested. And all this time she lived with Naomi.

One day, Naomi said to Ruth, "It's time I found you a husband, who will give you a home and take care of you. You have been picking up grain alongside the women who work for Boaz, and you know he is a relative of ours." She told Ruth to go to Boaz and remind him that it was his duty to take care of his kinfolk.

Boaz replied:

> The LORD bless you! This shows how truly loyal you are to your family. You could have looked for a younger man, either rich or poor, but you didn't. Don't worry, I'll do what you have asked. You are respected by everyone in town.

Boaz went and bought Naomi's property, and he married Ruth so that he could take care of both of them. The LORD blessed Ruth with a son. After his birth, the women said to Naomi:

> Praise the LORD! Today he has given you a grandson to take care of you. We pray that the boy will grow up to be famous everywhere in Israel.

And he did. The baby boy was named Obed, and he was the grandfather of the greatest king of all Israel, King David.

from **Ruth 1—4**

---

[a]*Moab:* The people of Moab worshiped idols and were usually the enemies of the people of Israel. [b]*Life . . . me:* Or "I'm sorry that the LORD has turned against me and made life so hard for you."

Samuel in the Temple

Elkanah and Hannah desperately wanted a child. Once a year Elkanah traveled from his hometown to Shiloh, where he worshiped the LORD All-Powerful and offered sacrifices. There Hannah prayed that the LORD would bless her with a son.

One time when Elkanah and Hannah went to Shiloh,

Hannah was crying as she prayed because she was so broken-hearted. She prayed, "LORD All-Powerful, I am your servant, but I am so miserable! Please let me have a son. I will give him to you as long as he lives."

Eli was one of the LORD's priests there, and he heard Hannah praying. Eli said to her, "You may go home now and stop worrying. I'm sure the God of Israel will answer your prayer."

Later, the LORD blessed Elkanah and Hannah with a

son. His name was Samuel. Just as Hannah had promised, when Samuel was a little older she gave her son back to the LORD. Samuel stayed in the temple in Shiloh with Eli and served the LORD.

Samuel served the LORD by helping Eli the priest, who was by that time almost blind. In those days, the LORD hardly ever spoke directly to people, and he did not appear to them in dreams very often. But one night, Eli was asleep in his room, and Samuel was sleeping on a mat near the sacred chest in the LORD's house. They had not been asleep very long[a] when the LORD called out Samuel's name.

"Here I am!" Samuel answered. Then he ran to Eli and said, "Here I am. What do you want?"

"I didn't call you," Eli answered. "Go back to bed."

Samuel went back.

Again the LORD called out Samuel's name. Samuel got up and went to Eli. "Here I am," he said. "What do you want?"

Eli told him, "Son, I didn't call you. Go back to sleep."

The LORD had not spoken to Samuel before, and Samuel did not recognize the voice. When the LORD called out his name for the third time, Samuel went to Eli again and said, "Here I am. What do you want?"

Eli finally realized that it was the LORD who was speaking to Samuel. So he said, "Go back and lie down! If someone speaks to you again, answer, 'I'm listening, LORD. What do you want me to do?' "

Once again Samuel went back and lay down.

The LORD then stood beside Samuel and called out as he had done before, "Samuel! Samuel!"

"I'm listening," Samuel answered. "What do you want me to do?"

The LORD said:

> Samuel, I am going to do something in Israel that will shock everyone who hears about it! I will punish Eli and his family, just as I promised. He knew that his sons refused to respect me,[b] and he let them get away with it, even though I said I would punish his family forever. I warned Eli that sacrifices or offerings could never make things right! His family has done too many disgusting things.

The next morning, Samuel got up and opened the doors to the LORD's house. He was afraid to tell Eli what the LORD had said. Eli called for Samuel.

"Here I am," Samuel answered.

Eli said, "What did God say to you? Tell me everything. I pray that God will punish you terribly if you don't tell me every word he said!"

Samuel told Eli everything. Then Eli said, "He is the LORD, and he will do what's right."

As Samuel grew up, the LORD helped him and made everything Samuel said come true.

from **1 Samuel 1; 3**

---

[a]*They . . . long:* The Hebrew text has "The lamp was still burning." An olive oil lamp would go out after a few hours if the wick were not adjusted. [b]*refused . . . me:* Or "were insulting everyone."

David and Goliath

David lived near Bethlehem with his father, Jesse, and his seven brothers. The LORD had chosen him to be special, and the Spirit of the LORD took control of him.

The enemies of Israel at that time were the Philistines. The Philistines got ready for war and brought their troops together to attack. The Israelites, under the command of King

Saul, set up camp on a hill near the Philistine camp. The Philistine army had a hero named Goliath who was from the town of Gath and was over nine feet[a] tall. He wore a bronze helmet and had bronze armor to protect his chest and legs. The chest armor alone weighed about one hundred twenty-five pounds. He carried a bronze sword strapped on his back, and his spear was so big that the iron spearhead alone weighed more than fifteen pounds.

Goliath went out and shouted to the army of Israel:

Why are you lining up for battle? I'm the best soldier in our army, and all of you are in Saul's army. Choose your best soldier to come out and fight me! If he can kill me, our people will be your slaves. Here and now I challenge Israel's whole army! Choose someone to fight me!

Saul and his men heard what Goliath said, but they were so frightened of Goliath that they couldn't do a thing.

David was Jesse's youngest son. He took care of his father's sheep, and he went back and forth between Bethelem and Saul's camp.

One day, Jesse told David, "Hurry and take this sack of roasted grain and these ten loaves of bread to your brothers at the army camp."

David obeyed his father. While he was in the army camp, Goliath came out from the line of Philistines and started boasting as usual. David heard him and asked why no one had gone to fight Goliath. Some soldiers overheard David talking, so they told Saul what David had said. Saul sent for David, and David offered to fight the giant.

"You don't have a chance against him," Saul replied. "You're only a boy, and he's been a soldier all his life."

But David told him, "The Lord has rescued me from the claws of lions and bears, and he will keep me safe from the hands of this Philistine."

Saul agreed to let David fight the giant. He even offered David his armor. But David refused it, taking only his sling and five smooth rocks.

When Goliath saw that David was just a healthy, good-looking boy, he made fun of him, and shouted, "Come on! When I'm finished with you, I'll feed you to the birds and wild animals!"

David answered:

> You've come out to fight me with a sword and a
> spear and a dagger. But I've come out to fight you in
> the name of the LORD All-Powerful.

When Goliath started forward, David ran toward him. He put a rock in his sling and swung the sling around by its straps. When he let go of one strap, the rock flew out and hit Goliath on the forehead. It cracked his skull, and he fell face-down on the ground. David defeated Goliath with a sling and a rock.

As David said, those who love God must never forget that the LORD doesn't need swords or spears to save his people. The LORD always wins his battles.

***from* 1 Samuel 16; 17**

ᵃ*over nine feet:* The Standard Hebrew Text; the Dead Sea Scrolls and some manuscripts of one ancient translation have "almost seven feet."

73

The Ethiopian Messenger

King David's son, Absalom, rebelled against his father and caused the Israelites to turn against the king's men in battle. David loved his son Absalom even though he had disobeyed and done wrong. Despite their differences, David made it clear that no one was to harm Absalom.

When Absalom saw that he would be defeated, he ran. He was riding his mule under a huge tree when his head[a]

caught in the branches. The mule ran off and left Absalom hanging in midair. Some of David's soldiers saw him and told Joab, who was in charge of David's army.

Joab said, "You saw Absalom? Why didn't you kill him?"

The man answered, "I wouldn't touch the king's son. We all heard King David tell you not to harm Absalom."

Joab was angry, and despite the king's orders, Joab killed Absalom for his rebellion against David.

Ahimaaz the son of Zadok said, "Joab, let me run and tell King David that the LORD has rescued him from his enemies."

But Joab knew that Ahimaaz only wanted to tell David in order to get attention. Joab answered, "You're not the one to tell the king that his son is dead. You can take him a message some other time, but not today."

An Ethiopian messenger was standing nearby. His tall, black, shiny body looked as if it were made for running. Everyone knew of his great running abilities. Joab told him, "Go and tell the king what you have seen." The man knelt down in front of Joab and then got up and started running.

Ahimaaz spoke to Joab again, "No matter what happens, I still want to run."

Joab explained to Ahimaaz that he'd receive no reward for telling the king the news.

"I'll run no matter what!" Ahimaaz insisted.

Joab finally agreed and let Ahimaaz run, too.

Ahimaaz took the road through the Jordan Valley and outran the Ethiopian.

Meanwhile, David was sitting between the inner and outer gates in the city wall.[b] One of his soldiers was watching from the roof of the gate-tower. He saw a man running toward the town and shouted down to tell David.

David answered, "If he's alone, he must have some news."

The runner was getting closer, when the soldier saw someone else running. He shouted down to the gate, "Look! There's another runner!"

David said, "He must have some news, too."

The soldier on the roof shouted, "The first one runs just like Ahimaaz the son of Zadok."

This time David said, "He's a good man. He must have some good news."

Ahimaaz called out, "We won! We won!" Then he bowed low to David and said, "Your Majesty, praise the LORD your God! He has given you victory over your enemies."

"Is my son Absalom all right?" David asked.

Ahimaaz said, "When Joab sent your personal servant and me, I saw a noisy crowd. But I don't know what it was all about."

David told him, "Stand over there and wait."

Ahimaaz went over and stood there. The Ethiopian came and said, "Your Majesty, today I have good news! The LORD has rescued you from all your enemies!'

"Is my son Absalom all right?" David asked.

The Ethiopian replied, "I wish that all Your Majesty's enemies and everyone who tries to harm you would end up like him!"

David started trembling. Then he went up to the room above the city gate to cry.

Ahimaaz had wanted the king's attention, but he refused to tell David the whole truth. Only the Ethiopian messenger had the courage to carry the bad news to the king.

2 Samuel 18.9–33a

---

a*head:* Or "hair." b*between . . . gates:* The city gate was often like a tower in the city wall, with one gate on the outside of the wall and another gate on the inside of the wall.

The Queen
of Sheba

King Solomon was a very rich king, and he was considered the wisest man in the world. The country of Israel was more important than ever before because of King Solomon.

The Queen of Sheba was a very beautiful and rich queen, who ruled a country to the south of Israel. The land of Sheba was known for the wonderful things, such as perfumes and incense, that it sold to the royal courts of other countries.

The Queen of Sheba had **heard how famous Solomon was, so she went to Jerusalem to test him with difficult questions.**

She took along several of her officials, and she loaded **79** her camels with gifts of spices, jewels, and gold. When she arrived, she and Solomon talked about everything she could think of. He answered every question, no matter how difficult it was.

The Queen was amazed at Solomon's wisdom. She was breathless when she saw his palace, the food on his table, his officials, his servants in their uniforms, the people who served his food, and the sacrifices he offered at the LORD's temple. She said:

Solomon, in my own country I had heard about your wisdom and all you've done. But I didn't believe it until I saw it with my own eyes! And there's so much I didn't hear about. You are wiser and richer than I was told. Your wives[a] and officials are lucky to be here where they can listen to the wise things you say.

I praise the LORD your God. He is pleased with you and has made you king of Israel. The LORD loves Israel, so he has given them a king who will rule fairly and honestly.

What a lesson this woman brings to us! Instead of being jealous and wanting what Solomon had, she praised God for all he had done for this wise king. She came from a country that was well-known for its treasures and spices, but she was pleased to see how God had blessed

Solomon.

The Queen of Sheba gave Solomon almost five tons of gold, many jewels, and more spices than anyone had ever brought into Israel.

In return, Solomon gave her the gifts he would have given any other ruler, but he also gave her everything else she wanted.

1 Kings 10.1–11

Elijah
and Elisha

Elijah was a great prophet of the LORD. He was obedient and did whatever the LORD asked him to do. He and Elisha traveled all over spreading the LORD's word.

One day Elijah said to Elisha, "The LORD wants me to

go to Bethel, but you must stay here." Elisha promised that
he would stay with Elijah no matter what. And he went with
Elijah to Bethel.

Elisha met a group of prophets in Bethel, and they
asked him, "Do you know that today the LORD is going to take
away your master?"

"Yes, I do," Elisha answered. "But don't remind me
of it."

Elijah then told Elisha that the LORD wanted him to   83 travel to Jericho. Again he told Elisha to stay behind. Elisha again promised never to leave his teacher's side. He traveled to Jericho with Elijah.

A group of prophets who lived there asked Elisha, "Do you know that today the LORD is going to take away your master?"

"Yes, I do," Elisha answered, "But don't remind me of it."

Elijah then said to Elisha, "Now the LORD wants me to go to the Jordan River, but you must stay here." Still again, Elisha promised never to leave Elijah. So the two of them walked on together.

Fifty prophets followed Elijah and Elisha from Jericho, then stood at a distance and watched as the two men walked toward the river. When they got there, Elijah took off his coat, then he rolled it up and struck the water with it. At once a path opened up through the river, and the two of them walked across on dry ground.

After they had reached the other side, Elijah said, "Elisha, the LORD will soon take me away. What can I do for you before that happens?"

Elisha answered, "Please give me twice as much of your power as you give the other prophets, so I can be the one who takes your place as their leader."

"It won't be easy," Elijah answered. "It can happen only if you see me as I am being taken away."

Elijah and Elisha were walking along and talking, when suddenly there appeared between them a flaming chariot pulled by fiery horses. Right away, a strong wind took Elijah up into heaven. After Elijah had gone, Elisha tore his clothes in sorrow.

Elijah's coat had fallen off, so Elisha picked it up and walked back to the Jordan River. He struck the water with the coat and wondered, "Will the LORD perform miracles for me as he did for Elijah?" As soon as Elisha did this, a dry path opened up through the water, and he walked across.

When the prophets from Jericho saw what happened, they said to each other, "Elisha now has Elijah's power." They walked over to him and bowed down.

2 Kings 2.1–11, 12b–15

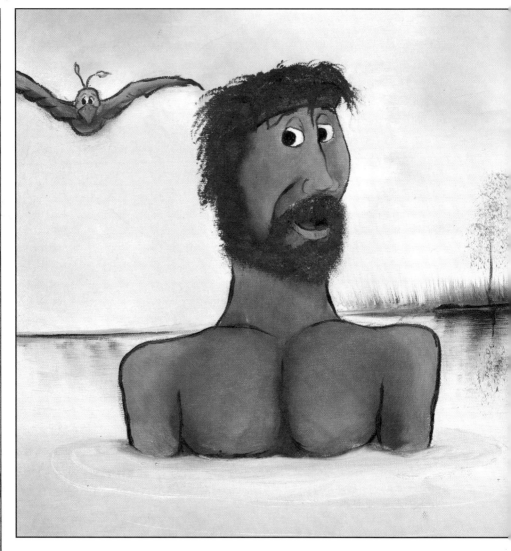

The Healing of Naaman

Naaman was the commander of the Syrian army. The LORD had helped him and his troops defeat their enemies, so the king of Syria respected Naaman very much. Naaman was a brave soldier, but he had a disease called leprosy.[a]

One day while the Syrian troops were raiding Israel, they captured a girl, and she became a servant of Naaman's wife. Some time later the girl said, "If your husband Naaman would go to the prophet[b] in Samaria, he would be cured of his leprosy." Clearly, God can use anyone, even a small girl, to give good news to those who need it.

So Naaman went to see Elisha the prophet. Naaman left with his horses and chariots and stopped at the door of Elisha's house. Elisha sent someone outside to say to him,

"Go wash seven times in the Jordan River. Then you'll be completely cured."

But Naaman stormed off, grumbling, "Why couldn't he come out and talk to me? I thought for sure he would stand in front of me and pray to the LORD his God, then wave his hand over my skin and cure me. Those rivers in Damascus are just as good as any river in Israel. I could have washed in them and been cured."

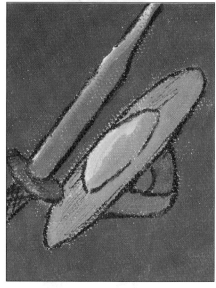

His servants went over to him and said, "Sir, if the prophet had told you to do something difficult, you would have done it. So why don't you do what he said? Go wash and be cured."

Naaman recognized this wisdom. He had not been told to do something hard in order to be healed. He needed only to obey.

Like Naaman, many of us think that obeying God means doing something hard. But just as Naaman was told to do something simple—wash in the river—we can obey God by doing simple things like praying, reading our Bible, keeping our promises, and believing that Jesus Christ is God's son. Obeying God is not hard. Naaman found this out, too.

Naaman walked down to the Jordan; he waded out into the water and stooped down in it seven times, just as Elisha had told him. Right away, he was cured, and his skin became as smooth as a child's.

Naaman and his officials went back to Elisha. Naaman stood in front of him and announced, "Now I know that the God of Israel is the only God in the whole world."

Naaman offered gifts to thank Elisha, but Elisha would not take them. He wanted Naaman to know that God had been the one who healed him, and he wanted Naaman to give gifts to the LORD. Naaman promised Elisha that he would give offerings only to the LORD from then on.

2 Kings 5.1–11, 12b–17

---

^a*leprosy:* The word translated "leprosy" was used for many different kinds of skin diseases. ^b*the prophet:* Hebrew "the man of God."

Nehemiah

Nehemiah was a Jewish man who worked for the king. He was in charge of all the wine used at the king's table. The king trusted and depended upon Nehemiah to keep careful watch over all his meals. This job made it possible for Nehemiah to see the king every day.

One day Nehemiah's brother came for a visit. He asked

his brother how things were in Jerusalem. Nehemiah's brother sadly told him the poor conditions of Jerusalem. The walls were all broken down, and the gates had been burned.

When Nehemiah heard all this, he sat down and cried. For days he mourned. He went without eating to show his sorrow and prayed:

Our Lord, I am praying for your servants—those you rescued by your great strength and mighty power. Please answer my prayer. . . . When I serve the king his wine today, make him pleased with me and have him do what I ask.

Later, when Nehemiah served wine to the king, the king noticed how sad Nehemiah looked. So the king said, "Why do you look so sad? You're not sick. Something must be bothering you."

Nehemiah, frightened, answered, "Your Majesty, I hope you live forever! I feel sad because the city where my ancestors are buried is in ruins, and its gates have been burned down."

The king asked, "What do you want me to do?" First, Nehemiah prayed to God in heaven, then told the king, "Sir, if it's all right with you, please send me back to Judah, so that I can rebuild the city where my ancestors are buried." The king agreed and sent Nehemiah back to Judah. He even prepared letters to the governors of all the places Nehemiah would travel through. This was to make sure Nehemiah would have a safe trip to Judah and a safe return. The king also sent along army officers and cavalry troops.

Nehemiah and his group set off for Judah. Sanballat and Tobiah heard about what happened and were very angry. They didn't want anyone to help the people of Israel.

Three days after arriving in Jerusalem, Nehemiah took a ride through the city. As he rode along, he took a good look at the crumpled walls of the city and the gates that had been torn down and burned. When he returned, he told the officials, "Jerusalem is truly in a mess! The gates have been torn down and burned, and everything is in ruins. We must rebuild the city wall so that we can again take pride in our city."

When Sanballat and Tobiah heard Nehemiah's plan to rebuild, they tore down his ideas with insults saying, "Just look at you! Do you plan to rebuild the walls of the city and rebel against the king?" Nehemiah answered, "We are servants of the God who rules from heaven, and he will make our work succeed."

Everyone helped rebuild the wall. When it was complete, Sanballat and Tobiah sent a message to Nehemiah asking him to meet them. Nehemiah sent a message back, "My work is too important to stop now and go there." They invited him four times, but each time he refused to go. Finally, Sanballat sent an official letter, which said: "A rumor is going around among the nations that you and the other Jews are rebuilding the wall and planning to rebel, because you want to be their king."

Nehemiah sent a message back to Sanballat, saying, "None of this is true! You are making it all up!"

Sanballat was indeed only trying to frighten Nehemiah. None of his claims were true. Nehemiah prayed that the LORD would punish Tobiah and Sanballat for what they had done.

The wall was completely rebuilt. When the enemies in the surrounding nations learned that the work was finished, they felt helpless, because they knew that God had helped rebuild the wall.

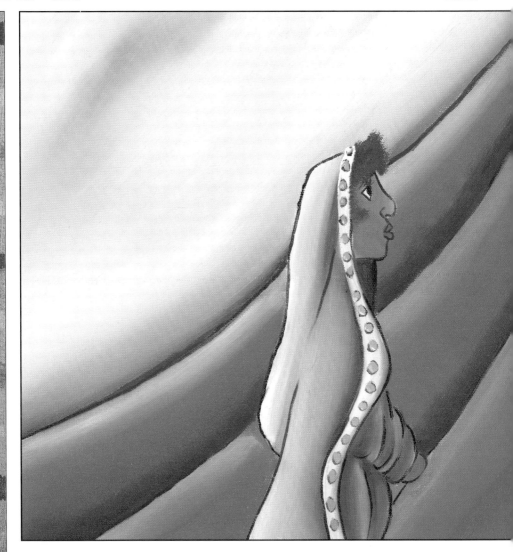

Esther

A Jewish man named Mordecai lived with his family in Persia. Mordecai had a very beautiful cousin named Esther. He had raised her as his own daughter, after her father and mother had died. When the king of Persia, King Xerxes, ordered the search for beautiful women, many were taken to the king's palace in Susa, and Esther was one of them. No one

knew Esther was a Jew because Mordecai had warned her not to tell anyone.

When the king met Esther, he fell in love with her right away and crowned her queen.

Mordecai had become a palace official and found out that two men who were in charge of guarding the king had decided to kill King Xerxes. Mordecai went to Queen Esther and asked her to warn the king. When King Xerxes found out that Mordecai's story was true, he had the two men killed.

Later, King Xerxes promoted Haman (who was a descendant of King Agag who had fought the Jews) to the highest position in his kingdom. The king had given orders for his officials at the royal gate to honor Haman by kneeling down to him. All of them obeyed except Mordecai.

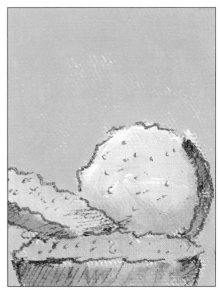

Haman was furious to learn that Mordecai refused to kneel down and honor him. And when he found out that Mordecai was a Jew, he knew that killing only Mordecai was not enough. Every Jew in the whole kingdom had to be killed.

Haman went to the king and suggested to him that the kingdom simply do away with all the Jewish people.

The king handed his official ring to Haman, who hated the Jews, and the king told him, "Do what you want with those people! You can keep their money."

Letters were written in the name of the king and sealed by using the king's own ring.[a] The letters were taken by messengers to every part of the kingdom, and this is what was said in the letters:

On the thirteenth day of Adar the twelfth month,
all Jewish men, women, and children are to be killed.
And their property is to be taken.

Mordecai told Esther's servant to tell Esther what Haman was planning and to ask her to beg the king to have pity on her people, the Jews.

The law said that Esther could not go to the king unless the king asked to see her. But Mordecai reminded her that if she didn't do something, she too would be put to death. "It could be that you were made queen for a time like this!" he said.

Esther had to do something to save her people, even if it meant her own death. So Esther dressed in her royal robes and went to see the king. He did not punish her, but was happy to see her and allowed her to come in. The king asked, "Esther, what brings you here? Just ask, and I will give you as much as half of my kingdom."

Esther did not tell the king right away why she had come to see him. Instead, she asked him to bring Haman to dinner. At dinner, the king again asked Esther what she wanted. This time Esther answered, "Your Majesty, if you really care for me and are willing to help, you can save me and my people. That evil Haman is the one out to get us!"

Haman was terrified as he looked at the king and queen. The king was very angry; he immediately ordered Haman killed.

Before the end of the day, the king gave Esther permission to make a law to save the lives of the Jewish people. After the law was announced, everyone in Susa shouted and cheered.

from **Esther 2.7—8.16**

---

^a*king's own ring:* Melted wax was used to seal a letter and while the wax was still soft, the king's ring was pressed in the wax to show that the letter was official.

Solomon and the Shulamite

King Solomon and the Shulamite woman were very much in love. They wanted to explain to each other and to their friends why they loved each other.

They wrote beautiful words to describe the feeling be-

tween them. This poem is a wonderful picture of love between husband and wife. They obviously respect and care for
each other in the way God meant for a husband and wife to
love each other.

He said to her:

My darling, you are lovely, so very lovely—
  your eyes are those of a dove . . .
My darling, when compared with other young
women,

you are a lily among thorns.

She told him:

I am yours, and you are mine.

On their wedding day, Solomon said to his wife:

My bride, my very own,
you have stolen my
heart!

You are a spring in the
garden, a fountain of
pure water,

and a refreshing
stream from Mount
Lebanon.

What if I could have
sixty queens, eighty
wives,

and thousands of others!

You would be my only choice, my flawless dove. . . .

Your charms are more powerful than all the stars
above.

The friends of Solomon and his wife found that it
was hard to understand the powerful feeling a man and a
woman can have for each other. So they asked the Shulamite
woman:

Most beautiful of women, why is the one you love
more special than others?

She tried to explain all the reasons that they could see:

He is handsome and healthy . . . his hair is wavy,
black as a raven . . . .

His legs are columns of marble on feet of gold.

She spoke of him, saying:

The passion of love bursting into flame
　　is more powerful than death, stronger than the
　　grave.
Love cannot be drowned by oceans or floods;
　　it cannot be bought, no matter what is offered.

And in the end, she explained that, most of all, he was her friend.

from Song of Songs 1—8

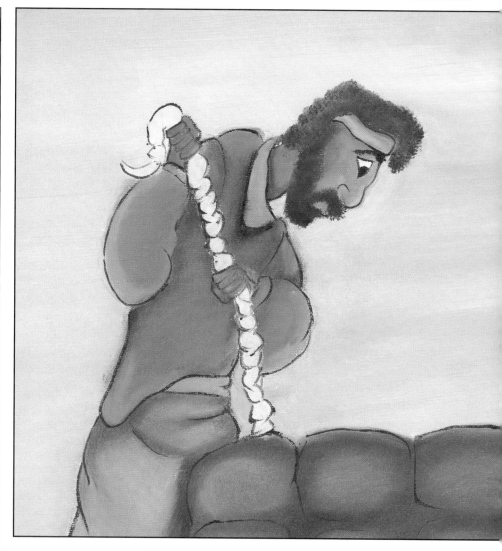

Ebedmelech

Jeremiah was a great prophet of God. He lived in Jerusalem and gave the people the messages that God had told him to give them.

When Jeremiah told them that the city would soon be defeated by their enemies, the people didn't like to hear what God had to say. They put Jeremiah in prison.

The king of Israel, King Zedekiah, liked Jeremiah, but he gave in to his officials, who didn't just want Jeremiah in prison—they wanted him to die! Four of them went to the king and said, "You should put Jeremiah to death, because he is making the soldiers and everyone else lose hope. He isn't trying to help our people; he's trying to harm them."

Zedekiah replied, "Do what you want with him. I can't stop you."

The four men took Jeremiah and used ropes to let him **103** down into a well that belonged to the king's son. There was no water in the well, and Jeremiah sank down in the mud.

Ebedmelech from Ethiopia[a] was an official at the palace, and he heard what they had done to Jeremiah. So he went to speak with King Zedekiah, who was holding court at Benjamin Gate.

Ebedmelech said, "Your Majesty, Jeremiah is a prophet, and those men were wrong to throw him into a well. And when Jerusalem runs out of food, Jeremiah will starve to death down there."

Zedekiah answered, "Take thirty[b] of my soldiers and pull Jeremiah out before he dies."

Ebedmelech and the soldiers went to the palace and got some rags from the room under the treasury. He used ropes to lower them into the well. Then he said to Jeremiah, "Put these rags under your arms so the ropes won't hurt you."

After Jeremiah did, the men pulled him out. And from then on, Jeremiah was kept in the courtyard of the palace guards.

Later, while Jeremiah was a prisoner in the courtyard of the palace guards, the LORD told him to say to Ebedmelech from Ethiopia:

I am the LORD, All-Powerful, the God of Israel. I warned everyone that I would bring disaster, not prosperity, to this city. Now very soon I will do what I said, and you will see it happen. But because you trusted me,[c] I will protect you from the officials of Judah, and when Judah is struck by disaster, I will rescue you and keep you alive. I, the LORD, have spoken.

God takes care of those who love and obey him.

Jeremiah 38.4–13; 39.15–18

[a]*Ethiopia:* The Hebrew text has "Cush," a region south of Egypt that included parts of the present countries of Ethiopia and Sudan. [b]*thirty:* Most Hebrew manuscripts; one Hebrew manuscript "three." [c]*you trusted me:* That is, Ebedmelech helped Jeremiah.

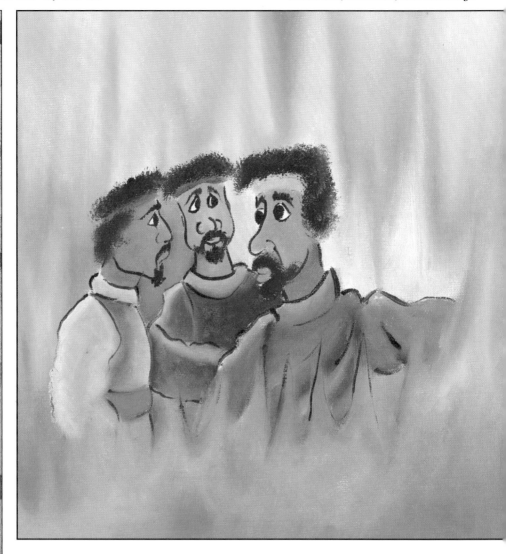

Shadrach, Meshach, and Abednego

King Nebuchadnezzar ordered a gold statue to be built ninety feet high and nine feet wide. He commanded that the people of every nation and race bow down and worship the statue. Anyone who refused would at once be thrown into

a flaming furnace. Everyone did as the king ordered, except for three men: Shadrach, Meshach, and Abednego.

King Nebuchadnezzar was furious. So he sent for the three young men and said, "I hear that you refuse to worship my gods and the gold statue I have set up. Now I am going to give you one more chance. If you bow down and worship the statue when you hear the music, everything will be all right. But if you don't, you will at once be thrown into a flaming furnace. No god can save you from me."

The three men replied, "Your Majesty, we don't need to defend ourselves. The God we worship can save us from you and your flaming furnace. But even if he doesn't we still won't worship your gods and the gold statue you have set up."

Nebuchadnezzar's face twisted with anger at the three men. And he ordered the furnace to be heated seven times hotter than usual. Next, he commanded some of his strongest soldiers to tie up the men and throw them into the flaming furnace. The king wanted it done at that very moment. So the soldiers tied up Shadrach, Meshach, and Abednego and threw them into the flaming furnace with all of their clothes on. The fire was so hot that flames leaped out and killed the soldiers.

Suddenly the king jumped up and shouted, "Weren't only three men tied up and thrown into the fire?"

"Yes, Your Majesty," the people answered.

"But I see four men walking around in the fire," the king replied. "None of them is tied up or harmed, and the fourth one looks like a god."[a]

Nebuchadnezzar went closer to the flaming furnace and said to the three young men, "You servants of the Most High God, come out at once!"

They came out, and the king's high officials, governors, and advisors all crowded around them. The men were not burned, their hair wasn't scorched, and their clothes didn't even smell like smoke. King Nebuchadnezzar said, "Praise their God for sending an angel to rescue his servants! They trusted their God and refused to obey my commands. Yes, they chose to die rather than to worship or serve any god except their own. And I won't allow people of any nation or race to say anything against their God. Anyone who does will be chopped up and their houses will be torn down because no other god has such great power to save."

After this happened, the king appointed Shadrach, Meshach, and Abednego to even higher positions in Babylon Province.

Daniel 3.1–3, 12–30

ᵃ*a god:* Aramaic, "a son of the gods."

Daniel
and the Lions' Den

D arius the Mede took over the kingdom of Babylon after King Belshazzar had been killed. Darius let Daniel govern the whole kingdom. Of course, this did not go over well with the other men. The other men tried to find something

wrong with the way Daniel did his work for the king. But they could not accuse him of anything wrong, because he was honest and faithful and did everything he was supposed to do. Finally, they said to one another, "We will never be able to bring any charge against Daniel, unless it has to do with his religion."

They all went to the king and said:

Your Majesty, you should make a law forbidding anyone to pray to any god or human except you for the next thirty days. Everyone who disobeys this law must be thrown into a pit of lions. Order this to be written and then sign it, so it cannot be changed.

So King Darius made the law and had it written down.

Daniel heard about the law, but when he returned home, he went upstairs and prayed in front of the window that faced Jerusalem. In the same way that he had always done, he knelt down in prayer three times a day, giving thanks to God.

The men who had spoken to the king watched Daniel and saw him praying to his God for help. They went back to the king and said, "Didn't you make a law that forbids anyone to pray to any god or human except you for the next thirty days? And doesn't the law say that everyone who disobeys it will be thrown into a pit of lions?"

"Yes, that's the law I made," the king agreed. The men told the king that Daniel refused to obey his law. Darius had no choice but to order that Daniel be thrown in the pit of lions. But he said to Daniel, "You have been faithful to your God, and I pray that he will rescue you."

A stone was rolled over the pit, and it was sealed. Then Darius and his officials stamped the seal to show that no one should let Daniel out. All night long the king could not sleep. He did not eat anything, and he would not let anyone come in to entertain him.

At daybreak, the king got up and ran to the pit. He was anxious and shouted, "Daniel, you were faithful and served your God. Was he able to save you from the lions?"

Daniel answered, "Your Majesty, I hope you live forever! My God knew that I was innocent, and he sent an angel to keep the lions from eating me. Your Majesty, I have never done anything to hurt you."

The king was relieved to hear Daniel's voice, and he gave orders for him to be taken out of the pit. Daniel's faith in his God had kept him from being harmed. And the king ordered the men who had brought charges against Daniel to be thrown into the pit.

King Darius then sent this message to all people of every nation and race in the world: "I command everyone in my kingdom to worship and honor the God of Daniel. He is the living God, the one who lives forever. His power and his kingdom will never end."

Daniel 5.30—6.26

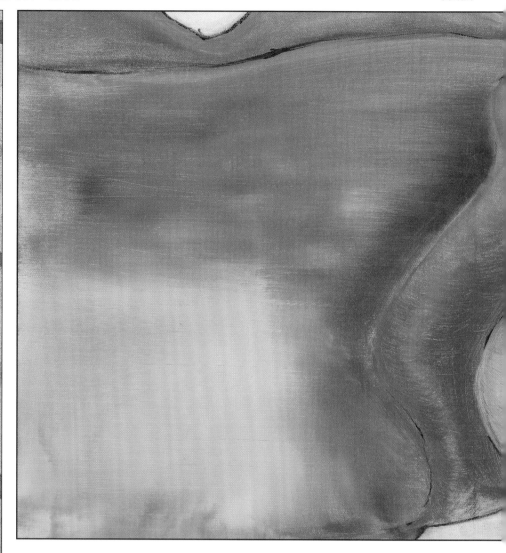

Jonah

One day the LORD told Jonah, the son of Amitai, to go to the great city of Nineveh[a] and say to the people, "The LORD has seen your terrible sins. You are doomed!"

Instead, Jonah ran from the LORD. He went to the seaport of Joppa and bought a ticket on a ship that was going to Spain. Then he got on the ship and sailed away to escape.

But the LORD made a strong wind blow, and such a bad

storm came up that the ship was about to be broken to pieces. The sailors were frightened, and they all started praying to their gods. They asked Jonah, "Are you the one who brought all this trouble on us?"

Jonah answered, "I'm a Hebrew, and I worship the LORD God of heaven, who made the sea and the dry land."

When the sailors heard this, they were frightened, because Jonah had already told them he was running from the LORD.

Then they said, "Do you know what you have done?" The storm kept getting worse, until finally the sailors asked him, "What should we do with you to make the sea calm down?"

Jonah told them, "Throw me into the sea, and it will calm down. I'm the cause of this terrible storm."

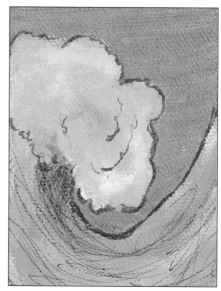

The sailors tried their best to row to the shore. But they could not do it, and the storm kept getting worse every minute. So they prayed to the LORD, "Please don't let us drown for taking this man's life. Don't hold us guilty for killing an innocent man. All of this happened because you wanted it to." Then they threw Jonah overboard, and the sea calmed down.

The LORD sent a big fish to swallow Jonah, and Jonah was inside the fish for three days and three nights.

Jonah was really in a bad situation. In the belly of a fish, at the bottom of the sea, Jonah prayed to the LORD and promised to do what the LORD told him to do. The LORD heard Jonah's prayers and commanded the fish to throw up Jonah onto the shore.

Once again the LORD told Jonah to go to that great city of Nineveh and preach his message of doom. This time Jonah obeyed the LORD. He went to Nineveh and warned the people of the LORD's plan to destroy their city. When the

king of Nineveh heard what was happening . . . he and his officials sent out an order for everyone in the city to obey. It said:

> None of you or your animals may eat or drink a thing . . . You must also pray to the LORD God with all your heart and stop being sinful and cruel. Maybe God will change his mind and have mercy on us, so we won't be destroyed.

When God saw that the people had stopped doing evil things, he had pity and did not destroy them as he had planned.

***from* Jonah 1.1—3.10**

[a]*Nineveh:* Capital city of Assyria, a hated enemy of Israel.

Mary
and Elizabeth

An angel of the Lord, Gabriel, appeared to Mary and Elizabeth to tell them that they would give birth to very special babies.

First, the angel told Elizabeth, who was very old and long past the age of having babies, that she and her husband

Zechariah would be blessed with a son, who would come to be known as John the Baptist. He would be a great servant of the Lord and would lead many people to salvation through the Lord, Jesus Christ.

One month later God sent the angel Gabriel to the town of Nazareth in Galilee with a message for a virgin named Mary. She was engaged to Joseph from the family of King David. The angel greeted Mary and said, "You are truly blessed. The Lord is with you."

Mary was confused by the angel's words and wondered what they meant. Then the angel told Mary, "Don't be afraid. God is pleased with you, and you will have a son. His name will be Jesus. He will be great and will be called the Son of God Most High. The Lord God will make him king, as his ancestor David was. He will rule the people of Israel forever, and his kingdom will never end."

Mary asked the angel, "How can this happen? I'm not married!"

The angel answered, "The Holy Spirit will come down to you, and God's power will come over you. So your child will be called the holy Son of God. Your relative Elizabeth is also having a son, even though she is old. No one thought she could ever have baby, but in three months she will have a son. Nothing is impossible for God!"

Mary said, "I am the Lord's servant! Let it happen as you have said." And the angel left her.

A short time later Mary hurried to a town in the hill country of Judea. She went into Zechariah's home, where she greeted Elizabeth. When Elizabeth heard Mary's greeting, her baby moved within her.

The Holy Spirit came upon Elizabeth. Then in a loud voice she said to Mary:

God has blessed you more than any other woman! He has also blessed the child you will have.

Why should the mother of my Lord come to me? As soon as I heard your greeting, my baby became happy and moved within me. The Lord has blessed you because you believed that he will keep his promise.

Mary said:

With all my heart I praise the Lord,
　　　and I am glad because of God my Savior.
God cares for me, his humble servant.
From now on, all people will say
　　　God has blessed me.
God All-Powerful has done great things for me,
　　　and his name is holy.
He always shows mercy
　　　to everyone who worships him.

Luke 1.11–50

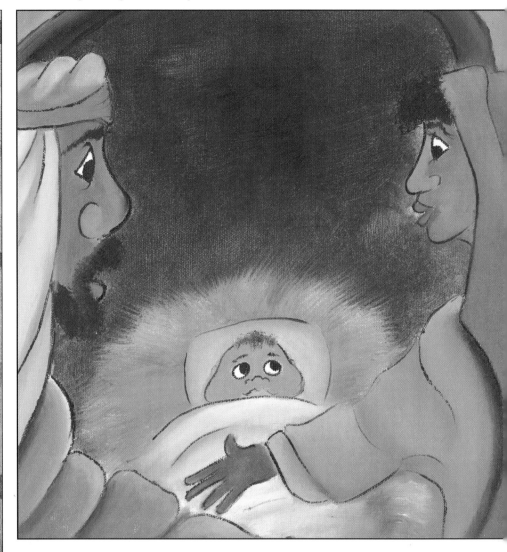

The Birth of Jesus

Emperor Augustus gave orders for the names of all the people to be listed in record books.[a] Everyone had to go to their own hometown to be listed. So Joseph had to leave Nazareth in Galilee and go to Bethlehem in Judea. Long ago Bethlehem had been King David's hometown, and Joseph went there because he was from David's family.

Mary was engaged to Joseph and traveled with him to Bethlehem. She was soon going to have a baby, and while they were there she gave birth to her first-born[b] son. She dressed him in baby clothes[c] and laid him on a bed of hay, because there was no room for them in the inn.

That night in the fields near Bethlehem some shepherds were guarding their sheep. All at once an angel came down to them from the Lord, and the brightness of the Lord's glory flashed around them. The shepherds were frightened.

123

But the angel said, "Don't be afraid! I have good news for you, which will make everyone happy. This very day in King David's hometown a Savior was born for you. He is Christ the Lord. You will know who he is, because you will find him dressed in baby clothes and lying on a bed of hay."

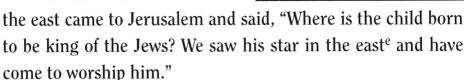

Suddenly many other angels came down from heaven and joined in praising God. They said:

"Praise God in heaven!
Peace on earth to
everyone who pleases
God."

Some wise men[d] from the east came to Jerusalem and said, "Where is the child born to be king of the Jews? We saw his star in the east[e] and have come to worship him."

When King Herod heard about this, he was worried, and so was everyone else in Jerusalem. Herod brought together the chief priests and the teachers of the Law of Moses and asked them, "Where will the Messiah be born?"

They told him, "He will be born in Bethlehem, just as the prophet wrote."

Herod secretly called in the wise men and asked them when they had first seen the star. He told them, "Go to Bethlehem and search carefully for the child. As soon as you find him, let me know. I want to go and worship him, too."

The wise men listened to what the king said and then left. And the star they had seen in the east went on ahead of them until it stopped over the place where the child was. They were thrilled and excited to see the star.

When the men went into the house and saw the child with Mary, his mother, they knelt down and worshiped him. They took out their gifts of gold, frankincense, and myrrh[f] and gave them to him. Later they were warned in a dream not to return to Herod, and they went back home by another road.

Matthew 2.1b–5, 7–15; Luke 2.1, 3–14

[a]*names . . . listed in record books:* This was done so that everyone could be made to pay taxes to the Emperor. [b]*first-born:* The Jewish people said that the first-born son in each of their families belonged to the Lord. [c]*dressed him in baby clothes:* The Greek text has "wrapped him in wide strips of cloth," which was how young babies were dressed. [d]*wise men:* People famous for studying the stars. [e]*his star in the east:* Or "his star rise." [f]*frankincense, and myrrh:* Frankincense was a valuable powder that was burned to make a sweet smell. Myrrh was a valuable sweet-smelling powder often used in perfume.

125

Jesus
Grows Up

After the wise men had gone, an angel from the Lord appeared to Joseph in a dream and said, "Get up! Hurry and take the child and his mother to Egypt! Stay there until I tell you to return, because Herod is looking for the child and wants to kill him."

That night, Joseph got up and took his wife and the child to Egypt where they stayed until King Herod died. So the Lord's promise came true, just as the prophet had said, "I called my son out of Egypt."

After King Herod died, an angel from the Lord appeared in a dream to Joseph while he was still in Egypt. The angel said, "Get up and take the child and his mother back to Israel. The people who wanted to kill him are now dead."

Joseph got up and left with them for Israel. But when

he heard that Herod's son Archelaus was now ruler of Judea, he was afraid to go there. Then in a dream he was told to go to Galilee, and they went to live there in the town of Nazareth.

The child Jesus grew. He became strong and wise, and God blessed him.

Every year Jesus' parents went to Jerusalem for Passover. And when Jesus was twelve years old, they  all went there as usual for the celebration. After Passover his parents left, but they did not know that Jesus had stayed on in the city.

They thought he was traveling with some other people, and they went a whole day before they started looking for him. When they could not find him with their relatives and friends, they went back to Jerusalem and started looking for him there.

Three days later they found Jesus in the temple, listening to the teachers and asking them questions. Everyone who heard him was surprised at how much he knew and at the answers he gave.

When his parents found him, they were amazed. His mother said, "Son, why have you done this to us? Your father and I have been very worried, and we have been searching for you!"

Jesus answered, "Why did you have to look for me?

Didn't you know that I would be in my Father's house?"[a] But they did not understand what he meant.

Jesus went back to Nazareth with his parents and obeyed them. His mother kept on thinking about all that had happened.

Jesus became wise, and he grew strong. God was pleased with him and so were the people.

Matthew 2.19–23: Luke 2.40–52

---

[a]*in my Father's house:* Or "doing my Father's work."

John the Baptist

John the Baptist started preaching in the desert of Judea. He said, "Turn back to God! The kingdom of heaven[a] will soon be here."[b]

John wore clothes made of camel's hair. He had a leather strap around his waist and ate grasshoppers and wild

honey.

From Jerusalem and all Judea and from the Jordan River Valley crowds of people went to John. They told him how sorry they were for their sins, and he baptized them in the river.

Many Pharisees and Sadducees also came to be baptized. But John said to them, "You bunch of snakes! Who warned you to run from the coming judgment? Do something to show that you have really given up your sins."

The crowds asked John, "What should we do?"

John told them, "If you have two coats, give one to someone who doesn't have any. If you have food, share it with someone else."

When tax collectors[c] came to be baptized, they asked John, "Teacher, what should we do?"

John told them, "Don't make people pay more than they owe."

Some soldiers asked him, "And what about us? What do we have to do?"

John told them, "Don't force people to pay money to make you leave them alone. Be satisfied with your pay."

Everyone became excited and wondered, "Could John be the Messiah?"

John said, "I am just baptizing with water. But someone more powerful is going to come, and I am not good enough even to untie his sandals.[d] He will baptize you with the Holy Spirit and with fire."

In many different ways John preached the good news to the people.

Jesus left Galilee and went to the Jordan River to be baptized by John. But John kept objecting and said, "I ought to be baptized by you. Why have you come to me?"

Jesus answered, "For now this is how it should be, because we must do all that God wants us to do." Then John agreed.

So Jesus was baptized. And as soon as he came out of the water, the sky opened, and he saw the Spirit of God coming down on him like a dove. Then a voice from heaven said, "This is my own dear Son, and I am pleased with him."

Matthew 3.1, 2, 4–7, 13–17; Luke 3.10–16, 18

[a]*kingdom of heaven:* In the Gospel of Matthew "kingdom of heaven" is used with the same meaning as "God's kingdom" in Mark and Luke. [b]*will soon be here:* Or "is already here." [c]*tax collectors:* These were usually Jewish people who paid the Romans for the right to collect taxes. They were hated by other Jews, who thought of them as traitors to their country and to their religion. [d]*untie his sandals:* This was the duty of a slave.

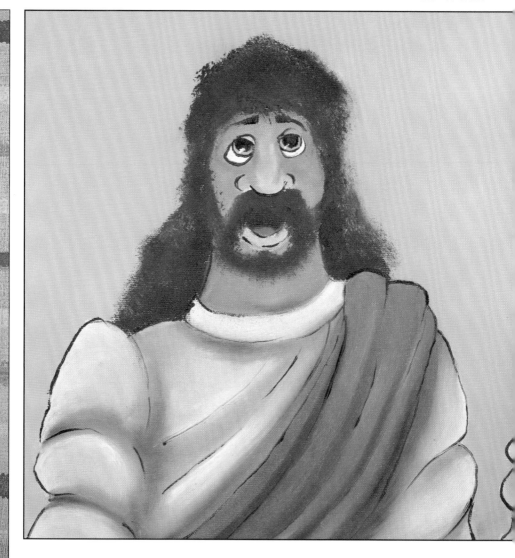

Water to Wine

Mary, the mother of Jesus, was at a wedding feast in the village of Cana in Galilee. Jesus and his disciples had also been invited and were there.

A wedding during the time of Jesus often lasted several days, with lots of parties. It was very important that the guests have enough food and wine. But halfway through this wedding, they ran out of wine. Mary knew that the people would be embarrassed. When the wine was all gone, Mary said to Jesus, "They don't have any more wine."

Jesus replied, "Mother, my time hasn't yet come!a You must not tell me what to do."

Mary then said to the servants, "Do whatever Jesus tells *135* you to do." She knew that Jesus would do the right thing and help out the people at the wedding.

At the feast there were six stone water jars that were used by the people for washing themselves in the way that their religion said they must. Each jar held about twenty or thirty gallons. Jesus told the servants to fill them to the top with water. Then after the jars had been filled, he said, "Now take some water and give it to the man in charge of the feast."

The servants did as Jesus told them, and the man in charge drank some of the water that had now turned into wine. He did not know where the wine had come from, but the servants did. He called the bridegroom over and said, "The best wine is always served first. Then after the guests have had plenty, the other wine is served. But you have kept the best until last!"

This was Jesus' first miracle,[b] and he did it in the village of Cana in Galilee. There Jesus showed his glory, and his disciples put their faith in him. After this, he went with his mother, his brothers, and his disciples to the town of Capernaum, where they stayed for a few days. Sometimes we think that sad times are the only times people think about God, but Jesus did this miracle—his first—at a party! Jesus enjoyed happy gatherings of people. He didn't preach at the wedding, but he did add to the joy there by supplying more wine. He did some very serious work later when he preached and taught and healed people. But Jesus knew that happy times are also good times to think about him.

John 2.1–12

[a]*my time hasn't yet come!:* The time when the true glory of Jesus would be seen, and he would be recognized as God's Son. [b]*miracle:* The Greek text has "sign." In the Gosepl of John the word "sign" is used for the miracle itself and as a way of pointing to Jesus as the Son of God.

Jesus' Disciples

Jesus was standing on the shore of Lake Gennesaret,[a] teaching the people as they crowded around him to hear God's message. Near the shore he saw two boats left there by some fishermen who had gone to wash their nets. Jesus got into the boat that belonged to Simon and asked him to row it out

a little way from the shore. Then Jesus sat down[b] in the boat to teach the crowd.

When Jesus had finished speaking, he told Simon, "Row the boat out into the deep water and let your nets down to catch some fish."

"Master," Simon answered, "we worked hard all night long and have not caught a thing. But if you tell me to, I will let the nets down." They did it and caught so many fish that their nets began ripping apart. Then they signaled for their

139

partners in the other boat to come and help them. The men came, and together they filled the two boats so full that they both began to sink.

When Simon Peter saw this happen, he knelt down in front of Jesus and said, "Lord, don't come near me! I am a sinner." Peter and everyone with him were completely surprised at all the fish they had caught. His partners, James and John, the sons of Zebedee, were surprised, too.

Jesus told Simon, "Don't be afraid! From now on you will bring in people instead of fish." The men pulled their boats up on the shore. Then they left everything and went with Jesus.

Jesus walked on until he saw James and John, the sons of Zebedee. They were in a boat with their father, mending their nets. Jesus asked them to come with him, too. Right away they left the boat and their father, and they went with Jesus.

As Jesus was leaving, he saw a tax collector[c] named Matthew sitting at the place for paying taxes. Jesus said to him, "Come with me." Matthew got up and went with him.

Later, Jesus and his disciples were having dinner at Matthew's house.[d] Many tax collectors and other sinners were also there. Some Pharisees asked Jesus' disciples, "Why does your teacher eat with tax collectors and other sinners?"

Jesus heard them and answered, "Healthy people don't

need a doctor, but sick people do. Go and learn what the Scriptures mean when they say, 'Instead of offering sacrifices to me, I want you to be merciful to others.' I didn't come to invite good people to be my followers. I came to invite sinners."

Jesus decided to ask some of his disciples to go up on a mountain with him, and they went. Then he chose twelve of them to be his apostles,[e] so that they could be with him. He also wanted to send them out to preach and to force out demons. Simon was one of the twelve, and Jesus named him Peter. There were also James and John, the two sons of Zebedee. They talked so much and so loudly that Jesus gave them a nickname that meant "Thunderbolts." Andrew, Philip, Bartholomew, Matthew, Thomas, James the son of Alphaeus, and Thaddaeus were also apostles. The others were Simon, known as the Eager One,[f] and Judas Iscariot,[g] who later betrayed Jesus.

Matthew 4.21,22; 9.9–13; Mark 3.13–19; Luke 5.1–11

[a]*Lake Gennesaret:* Another name for Lake Galilee. [b]*sat down:* Teachers in the ancient world, including Jewish teachers, usually sat down when they taught. [c]*tax collector:* These were usually Jewish people who paid the Romans for the right to collect taxes. They were hated by other Jews, who thought of them as traitors to their country and to their religion. [d]*Matthew's house:* Or "Jesus' house." [e]*to be his apostles:* These words are not in some manuscripts. [f]*known as the Eager One:* The Greek text has "Cananaean," which probably comes from a Hebrew word meaning "zealous." "Zealot" was the name later given to the members of a Jewish group which resisted and fought against the Romans. [g]*Iscariot:* This may mean "a man from Kerioth (a place in Judea). But more probably it means "a man who was a liar" or "a man who was a betrayer."

Jesus Feeds
Five Thousand

Jesus had sent the apostles out to teach people about God.
When they returned, they told him everything they had
done and taught. But so many people were coming and
going that Jesus and the apostles did not even have a chance
to eat.

Then Jesus said, "Let's go to a place[a] where we can be alone and get some rest." They left in a boat for a place where they could be alone. But many people saw them leave and figured out where they were going. So people from every town ran on ahead and got there first.

When Jesus got out of the boat, he saw the large crowd that was like sheep without a shepherd. He felt sorry for the people and started teaching them many things.

That evening the disciples came to Jesus and said, *143*

"This place is like a desert, and it is already late. Let the crowds leave, so they can go to the farms and villages near here and buy something to eat."

Jesus replied, "You give them something to eat."

But they asked him, "Don't you know that it would take almost a year's wages[b] to buy all of these people something to eat?"

Then Jesus said, "How much bread do you have? Go and see!"

Andrew, the brother of Simon Peter, was one of the disciples. He spoke up and said, "There a boy here who has five small loaves[c] of barley bread and two fish. But what good is that with all these people?"

Jesus told his disciples to have the people sit down on the green grass. They sat down in groups of a hundred and groups of fifty.

Jesus took the five loaves and the two fish. He looked up toward heaven and blessed the food. Then he broke the bread and handed it to his disciples to give to the people. He also divided the two fish, so that everyone could have some.

After everyone had eaten all they wanted, Jesus' disciples picked up twelve large baskets of leftover bread and fish.

There were about five thousand men who ate, not counting the women and children.

After the people had seen Jesus work this miracle, they

began saying, "This must be the Prophet[d] who is to come into the world!" Jesus realized that they would try to force him to be their king. So he went up on a mountain, where he could be alone.

Matthew 14.21; Mark 6.30–43; John 6.8, 9, 14, 15

[a] *a place:* This was probably northeast of Lake Galilee. [b] *almost a year's wages:* The Greek text has "two hundred silver coins." Each coin was the average day's wage for a worker. [c] *small loaves:* These would have been flat and round or in the shape of a bun. [d] *the Prophet:* Many of the Jewish people expected God to send them a prophet who would be like Moses, but with even greater power.

Sermon
on the Mount

Thousands came to hear Jesus' Sermon on the Mount. When Jesus saw the crowds, he went up on the side of a mountain and sat down.[a]

Jesus' disciples gathered around him, and he taught them. This is what Jesus said:

God blesses those people
    who depend only on him.
They belong to the kingdom
    of heaven!^b
God blesses those people who grieve.
    They will find comfort!
God blesses those people
    who are humble.

The earth will belong
to them!
God blesses those people who want to obey him[c]
more than they like to eat or drink.
They will be given
what they want!
God blesses those people
who are merciful.
They will be treated
with mercy!
God blesses those people
whose hearts are
pure.
They will see him!
God blesses those people
who make peace.
They will be called
his children!
God blesses those people who are treated badly
for doing right.
They belong to the kingdom
of heaven.

God will bless you when people insult you, mistreat you, and tell all kinds of evil lies about you because of me. Be happy and excited! You will have a great reward in heaven! People did these same things to the prophets who lived long ago.

You are like salt for everyone on earth. But if salt no longer tastes like salt, how can it make food salty? All it is good for is to be thrown out and walked on.

You are like light for the whole world. A city built on top of a hill cannot be hidden, and no one would light a lamp and put it under a clay pot. A lamp is placed on a lampstand, where it can give light to everyone in the house. Make your light shine, so that others will see the good that you do and will praise your Father in heaven.

Matthew 5.1–16

a*sat down:* Teachers in the ancient world, including Jewish teachers, usually sat down when they taught. b*They belong to the kingdom of heaven:* Or "The kingdom of heaven belongs to them." c*who want to obey him:* Or "who want to do right" or "who want everyone to be treated right."

Stories Jesus Told

At the end of his Sermon on the Mount, Jesus suggested that everyone take a good look at their lives and try to live according to God's law. He told several stories that showed people how to live.

Jesus said:

When you do good deeds, don't try to show off. If

you do, you won't get a reward from your Father in heaven.

When you give to the poor, don't blow a loud horn. That's what show-offs do in the meeting places and on the street corners, because they are always looking for praise. I can assure you that they already have their reward.

When you give to the poor, don't let anyone know about it.[a] Then your gift will be given in secret.

151

Your Father knows what is done in secret, and he will reward you.

Don't judge others, and God won't judge you. Don't be hard on others, and God won't be hard on you. Forgive others, and God will forgive you. If you give to others, you will be given a full amount in return. It will be packed down, shaken together, and spilling over into your lap. The way you treat others is the way you will be treated.

Love your enemies, and be good to everyone who hates you. Ask God to bless anyone who curses you, and pray for everyone who is cruel to you.

If you love only someone who loves you, will God praise you for that? Even sinners love people who love them. But love your enemies and be good to them. Lend without expecting to be paid back.[b] Then you will get a great reward, and you will be the true children of God in heaven.

Anyone who hears and obeys these teachings of mine is like a wise person who built a house on solid rock. Rain poured down, rivers flooded, and winds beat against that house. But it did not fall, because it was built on solid rock.

Anyone who hears my teachings and doesn't

obey them is like a foolish person who built a house on sand. The rain poured down, the rivers flooded, and the winds blew and beat against that house. Finally, it fell with a crash.

When Jesus finished speaking, the crowds were surprised at his teaching. He taught them like someone with authority, and not like their teachers of the Law of Moses. All who heard had a choice to make.

Matthew 6.1–4; 7.24–29; Luke 6.27, 32, 35, 37, 38

---

[a]*don't let anyone know about it:* The Greek text has, "Don't let your left hand know what your right hand is doing." [b]*without expecting to be paid back:* Some manuscripts have "without giving up on anyone."

The Mustard Seed

The next time Jesus taught beside Lake Galilee, a big crowd gathered. It was so large that he had to sit in a boat out on the lake, while the people stood on the shore. He used stories to teach them many things, and this is part of what he taught:

Now listen! A farmer went out to scatter seed in a field. While the farmer was scattering the seed, some of it fell along the road and was eaten by birds. Other seeds fell on thin, rocky ground and quickly started growing because the soil wasn't very deep. But when the sun came up, the plants were scorched and dried up, because they did not have enough roots. Some other seeds fell where thorn-bushes grew up and choked out the plants. So they did not produce any grain. But a few seeds did fall on good ground where the plants grew and produced thirty or sixty or even a hundred times as much as was scattered.

Then Jesus said, "If you have ears, pay attention."

When Jesus was alone with the twelve apostles and some others, they asked him about these stories. He answered:

I have explained the secret about God's kingdom to you, but for others I can use only stories. The reason is,

"These people will look and look, but never see.
They will listen and listen, but never understand.
If they did, they would turn to God,
and he would forgive them."

Jesus told them:

If you don't understand this story, you won't understand any others. What the farmer is spreading is really the message about the kingdom. The seeds that fell along the road are the people who hear the message. But Satan soon comes and snatches it away from them. The seeds that fell on rocky ground are the people who gladly hear the message and accept it right away. But they don't have any roots, and they don't last very long. As soon as life gets hard or the message gets them in trouble, they give up.

The seeds that fell among the thornbushes are also people who hear the message. But they start worrying about the needs of this life. They are fooled by the desire to get rich and to have all kinds of other things. So the message gets choked out, and they never produce anything. The seeds that fell on good ground are the people who hear and welcome the message. They produce thirty or sixty or even a hundred times as much as was planted.

Finally, Jesus said:

What is God's kingdom like? What story can I use to explain it? It is like what happens when a mustard seed is planted in the ground. It is the smallest seed in all the world. But once it is planted, it grows larger than any garden plant. It even puts out branches that are big enough for birds to nest in its shade.

Jesus used many other stories when he spoke to the people, and he taught them as much as they could understand. He did not tell them anything without using stories. But when he was alone with his disciples, he explained everything to them.

Mark 4.1–20, 30–34

Jesus Walks on the Water

After Jesus had fed the five thousand, his disciples got into a boat to cross over the lake to Bethsaida. But he stayed until he had sent the crowds away. Then he told them good-by and went up on the side of a mountain to pray.

Later that same evening, Jesus was still on the moun-

tain alone. By this time the boat was a long way from the shore, somewhere in the middle of the lake. It was going against the wind and was being tossed around by the waves. The disciples were struggling very hard to keep control of the boat against the strong winds.

A little while before morning, Jesus came walking on the water toward his disciples. When they saw him, they thought he was a ghost. They were terrified and started screaming.

At once, Jesus said to them, "Don't worry! I am Jesus. Don't be afraid."

Peter replied, "Lord, if it is really you, tell me to come to you on the water."

"Come on!" Jesus said. Peter then got out of the boat and started walking on the water toward him.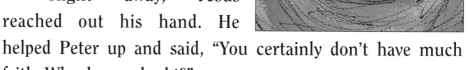

But when Peter saw how strong the wind was, he was afraid and started sinking. "Save me, Lord!" he shouted.

Right away, Jesus reached out his hand. He helped Peter up and said, "You certainly don't have much faith. Why do you doubt?"

When Jesus and Peter got into the boat, the wind died down. The men in the boat worshiped Jesus and said, "You really are the Son of God!"

Jesus and his disciples crossed the lake and came to shore near the town of Gennesaret. As soon as they got out of the boat, the people recognized Jesus.

The people who had stayed on the east side of the lake knew that only one boat had been there. They also knew that Jesus had not left in it with his disciples. But the next day some boats from Tiberias sailed near the place where the crowd had eaten the bread for which the Lord had given thanks. They saw that Jesus and his disciples had left. Then they got into the boats and went to Capernaum to look for Jesus. They found him on the west side of the lake and asked, "Rabbi, when did you get here?"

Jesus answered, "I tell you for certain that you are not looking for me because you saw the miracles,[a] but because you ate all the food you wanted. Don't work for food that spoils. Work for food that gives eternal life. The Son of Man will give you this food, because God the Father has given him the right to do so."

The people said, "Lord, give us this bread and don't ever stop!"

Jesus replied:

I am the bread that gives life! No one who comes to me will ever be hungry. No one who has faith in me will ever be thirsty. I have told you already that you have seen me and still do not have faith in me. Everything and everyone that the Father has given me will come to me, and I won't turn any of them away.

But the people still came to Jesus, not to believe in him as the Son of God, but so that he could heal them and perform other miracles. So they ran all over that part of the country to bring their sick people to him. They brought them each time they heard where he was. In every village or farm or marketplace where Jesus went, the people brought their sick to him. They begged him to let them just touch his clothes, and everyone who did was healed.

Matthew 14.22–36; John 6.22–27, 34–37

[a]*miracles:* The Greek text has "sign" here.

The Good Samaritan

When Jesus spoke to his disciples, he tried to explain to them how special they were to be able to be with Jesus and hear his teachings. Many people, even those who had studied the Scriptures for a long time, could not understand what Jesus was talking about. Instead, Jesus wanted to make

sure that ordinary people could hear and understand his messages.

At that same time, Jesus felt the joy that comes from the Holy Spirit,[a] and he said:

My Father, Lord of heaven and earth, I am grateful that you hid all this from wise and educated people and showed it to ordinary people. Yes, Father, that is what pleased you.

My Father has given me everything, and he is the

163

only one who knows the Son. The only one who really knows the Father is the Son. But the Son wants to tell others about the Father, so that they can know him too.

Jesus then turned to his disciples and said to them in private, "You are really blessed to see what you see! Many prophets and kings were eager to see what you see and to hear what you hear. But I tell you that they did not see or hear."

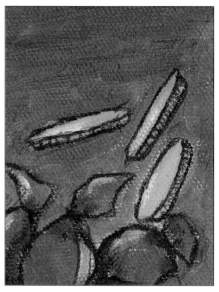

An expert in the Law of Moses stood up and asked Jesus a question to see what he would say. "Teacher," he asked, "what must I do to have eternal life?"

Jesus answered, "What is written in the Scriptures? How do you understand them?"

The man replied, "The Scriptures say, 'Love the Lord your God with all your heart, soul, strength, and mind.' They also say, 'Love your neighbors as much as you love yourself.' "

Jesus said, "You have given the right answer. If you do this, you will have eternal life."

But the man wanted to show that he knew what he was talking about. So he asked Jesus, "Who are my neighbors?"

Jesus replied:

As a man was going down from Jerusalem to Jericho, robbers attacked him and grabbed everything he had. They beat him up and ran off, leaving him half dead.

A priest happened to be going down the same road. But when he saw the man, he walked by on the other side. Later a temple helper[b] came to the same place. But when he saw the man who had been beaten up, he also went by on the other side.

A man from Samaria then came traveling along that road. When he saw the man, he felt sorry for him and went over to him. He treated his wounds with olive oil and wine[c] and bandaged them. Then he put him on his own donkey and took him to an inn, where he took care of him. The next morning he gave the innkeeper two silver coins and said, "Please take care of the man. If you spend more than this on him, I will pay you when I return.

Then Jesus asked, "Which one of these three people was a real neighbor to the man who was beaten up by robbers?"

The teacher answered, "The one who showed pity."

Jesus said, "Go and do the same!"

Luke 10.25–37

[a]*the Holy Spirit:* Some manuscripts have "his spirit." [b]*temple helper:* A man from the tribe of Levi, whose job it was to work around the temple. [c]*olive oil and wine:* In New Testament times these were used as medicine. Sometimes olive oil is a symbol for healing by means of a miracle.

Mary and Martha

Often Jesus told his disciples and the people around them not to become too caught up in what was going on around them. Money, good clothes, toys, and big houses were not as important as obeying God and learning all that Jesus had to say.

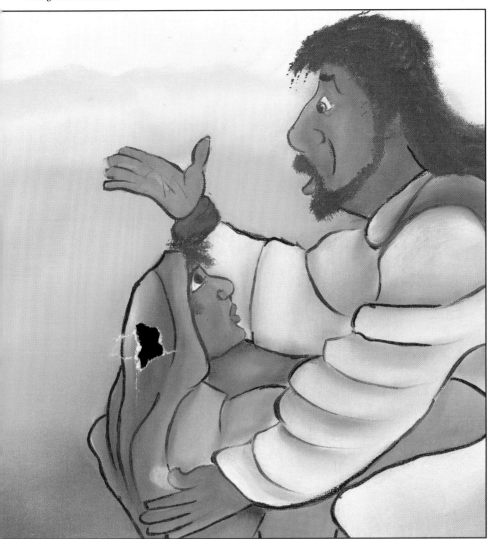

He told them, "Make sure that your treasure is safe in heaven, where thieves cannot steal it and moths cannot destroy it. Your heart will always be where your treasure is."

He meant that if you always put God first in your mind, then your heart will tell you the right things to do. He taught this often, sometimes even to his closest friends.

For example, when the Lord and his disciples were traveling along, they came to the village of Bethany. There he stayed with some friends.

Martha, her sister Mary, and their brother Lazarus were all good friends to Jesus and were very special to him.

While Jesus was visiting, Mary sat down at Jesus' feet and listened to everything that Jesus said.

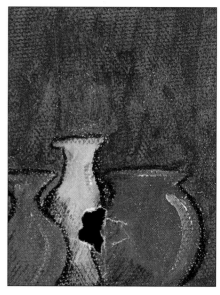

Martha, like her sister, was very excited that Jesus was visiting, but she knew how important it was to make sure that Jesus and all his disciples were comfortable and well fed. Martha was one of those special women who have a gift for making people feel loved and welcomed in her home. She enjoyed having Jesus and his disciples in her home, and she worked hard to make sure they had all they needed. She wanted everything to be just right.

Martha was worried about all that had to be done. The house needed to be cleaned, and food had to be prepared. Martha was a good hostess, but she would have liked to have had some help.

Martha was unhappy because her sister Mary continued to sit and listen to Jesus without helping her with any of the housework.

Finally, she went to Jesus and said, "Lord, doesn't it bother you that my sister has left me to do all the work by myself? Tell her to come and help me."

The Lord answered, "Martha, Martha! You are worried

and upset about so many things, but only one thing is necessary. Mary has chosen what is best, and it will not be taken away from her."

Martha understood. She relaxed and smiled. Although her duties were very important, she learned that the most important thing was to hear Jesus' words.

Luke 10.38–42; 12.33, 34

Being Lost

All kinds of people who had sinned were crowded around Jesus, including tax collectors, who were considered some of the worst sinners.

The officials and others who held high places in the temple began to whisper about Jesus being friendly to these sinners. He even ate with them!

About this time the disciples came to Jesus and asked him who would be the greatest in the kingdom of heaven. Jesus called a child over and had the child stand near him. Then he said:

I promise you this. If you don't change
and become like a child, you will never get into
the kingdom of heaven. But if you are as humble

as this child, you are the greatest in the kingdom of heaven. And when you welcome one of these children because of me, you welcome me.

Don't be cruel to any of these little ones! I promise you that their angels are always with my Father in heaven.[a] Let me ask you this.

If any of you has a hundred sheep, and one of them gets lost, what will you do? Won't you leave the ninety-nine in the field and go look for the lost sheep until you find it? And when you find it, you will be so glad that you will put it on your shoulder and carry it home. Then you will call in your friends and neighbors and say, "Let's celebrate! I've found my lost sheep!"

Jesus said, "In the same way there is more happiness in heaven because of one sinner who turns to God than over ninety-nine good people who don't need to."

Jesus told the people another story:

What will a woman do if she has ten silver coins and loses one of them? Won't she light a lamp, sweep the floor, and look carefully until she finds it? Then she will call in her friends and neighbors and say, "Let's celebrate! I've found the coin I lost."

Jesus said, "In the same way God's angels are happy when even one person turns to him."

Matthew 18.1–5, 10–12; Luke 15.1–10

[a]*in heaven:* Some manuscripts add, "The Son of Man came to save people who are lost."

Raising Lazarus

A man by the name of Lazarus was sick in the village of Bethany. He had two sisters, Mary and Martha. The sisters sent a message to the Lord and told him that his good friend Lazarus was sick.

When Jesus heard this, he said, "His sickness won't end in death. It will bring glory to God and his Son."

Jesus loved Martha and her sister and brother. But he stayed where he was for two more days. Then he said to his disciples, "Now we will go back to Judea." Then he told them, "Our friend Lazarus is asleep, and I am going to wake him up."

They replied, "Lord, if he is asleep, he will get better." Jesus really meant that Lazarus was dead, but they thought he was talking only about sleep.

Then Jesus told them plainly, "Lazarus is dead! I am   *175* glad that I wasn't there, because now you will have a chance to put your faith in me. Let's go to him."

When Jesus got to Bethany, he found that Lazarus had already been in the tomb four days. Bethany was only about two miles from Jerusalem, and many people had come from the city to comfort Martha and Mary because their brother had died.

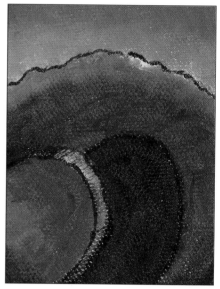

When Martha heard that Jesus had arrived, she went out to meet him, but Mary stayed in the house. Martha said to Jesus, "Lord, if you had been here, my brother would not have died. Yet even now I know that God will do anything you ask."

Jesus told her, "Your brother will live again!"

Martha answered, "I know that he will be raised to life on the last day,[a] when all the dead are raised."

Jesus then said, "I am the one who raises the dead to life! Everyone who has faith in me will live, even if they die. And everyone who lives because of faith in me will never really die. Do you believe this?"

"Yes, Lord!" she replied.

Mary, too, went to see Jesus. Many people had come to comfort Mary, and when they saw her quickly leave the house, they thought she was going out to the tomb to cry. So they followed her.

When Jesus saw that Mary and the people with her

were crying, he was terribly upset and asked, "Where have you put his body?"

They replied, "Lord, come and you will see."

Jesus started crying, and the people said, "See how much he loved Lazarus."

Some of them said, "He gives sight to the blind. Why couldn't he have kept Lazarus from dying?"

Jesus was still terribly upset. So he went to the tomb, which was a cave with a stone rolled against the entrance. Then he told the people to roll the stone away. But Martha said, "Lord, you know that Lazarus has been dead four days, and there will be a bad smell."

Jesus replied, "Didn't I tell you that if you had faith, you would see the glory of God?"

After the stone had been rolled aside, Jesus looked up toward heaven and prayed, "Father, I thank you for answering my prayer. I know that you always answer my prayers. But I said this, so that the people here would believe that you sent me."

When Jesus had finished praying, he shouted, "Lazarus, come out!" The man who had been dead came out. His hands and feet were wrapped with strips of burial cloth, and a cloth covered his face.

Jesus then told the people, "Untie him and let him go."

Many of the people who had come to visit Mary saw the things that Jesus did, and they put their faith in him.

John 11.1–7, 11–15, 17–27, 31, 33–45

ᵃ*the last day:* When God will judge all people.

A Rich Fool

Jesus often told his disciples and the others around him that people who love and follow God should not spend time thinking about money or other things they think they need. God will make sure we have everything we need.

After all, God provides food for even the smallest of animals. If he cares about a small bird like a sparrow, then think

how much more he cares for his children—those who love him.

Jesus said to his disciples:

I tell you not to worry about your life! Don't worry about having something to eat or wear. Life is more than food or clothing. Look at the crows! They don't plant or harvest, and they don't have storehouses or barns. But God takes care of them. You are much more important than any birds.

Can worry make you live longer?[a] If you don't have power over small things, why worry about everything else?

Look how the wild flowers grow! They don't work hard to make their clothes. But I tell you that Solomon with all his wealth[b] wasn't as well clothed as one of these flowers. God gives such beauty to everything that grows in the fields, even though it is here today and thrown into a fire tomorrow. Won't he do 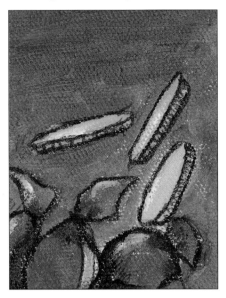 even more for you? You have such little faith! Don't keep worrying about having something to eat or drink. Only people who don't know God are always worrying about such things. Your Father knows what you need. But put God's work first, and these things will be yours as well.

Jesus was teaching a crowd when a man said to him, "Teacher, tell my brother to give me my share of what our father left us when he died."

Jesus answered, "Who gave me the right to settle arguments between you and your brother?"

Then he said to the crowd, "Don't be greedy! Owning a lot of things won't make your life safe."

So Jesus told them this story:

A rich man's farm produced a big crop, and he

said to himself, "What can I do? I don't have a place large enough to store everything."

Later, he said, "Now I know what I'll do. I'll tear down my barns and build bigger ones, where I can store all my grain and other goods. Then I'll say to myself, 'You have stored up enough good things to last for years to come. Live it up! Eat, drink, and enjoy yourself!' "

But God said to him, "You fool! Tonight you will die. Then who will get what you have stored up?"

Jesus told the crowd, "This is what happens to people who store up everything for themselves, but are poor in the sight of God."

Luke 12.13–31

^a*live longer:* Or "grow taller." ^b*Solomon with all his wealth:* The Jewish people thought that Solomon was the richest person who had ever lived.

Zacchaeus

Jesus was going through Jericho, where a man named Zacchaeus lived. He was in charge of collecting taxes[a] and was very rich.

Tax collectors then were not like tax collectors today.

In Jesus' time, tax collectors were people who paid for the

right to collect taxes. They often made money by cheating people. They charged them too much and kept what they didn't have to pay to the government.

Most people hated tax collectors. They thought of them as traitors to their country and to their religion. They were thought of as sinners. But this sinner was determined to see Jesus and to hear what he was teaching.

Jesus was heading his way, and Zaccheus wanted to see what he was like. But Zaccheus was a short man and could not see over the crowd. So he ran ahead and climbed up into a sycamore tree.

When Jesus got there, he looked up and said, "Zacchaeus, hurry down! I want to stay with you today." Zacchaeus hurried down and gladly welcomed Jesus.

Everyone who saw this started grumbling, "This man Zacchaeus is a sinner! And Jesus is going home to eat with him!"

Later that day Zacchaeus stood up and said to the Lord, "I will give half of my property to the poor. And I will now pay back four times as much[b] to everyone I have ever cheated."

This was amazing! No one had ever heard of a tax collector paying back money, much less four times as much. This was a sign that Zacchaeus was truly sorry for all he had done wrong.

Jesus said to Zacchaeus, "Today you and your family have been saved,[c] because you are a true son of Abraham.[d] The Son of Man came to look for and to save people who are lost."

As a tax collector who had cheated people, Zacchaeus had probably gotten very rich, but he was lost from God. But when he came to know Jesus, he became a new man. When he believed in Jesus as the Son of God, and when he believed what Jesus had taught him, he grew close to God again.

But Zacchaeus knew that real faith is not only believing and loving Jesus. It means that he had to turn from his old way of doing things—cheating and lying—and obey all God's commands. Real faith acts to make things right again.

Luke 19.1–9

ᵃ*in charge of collecting taxes:* These were usually Jewish people who paid the Romans for the right to collect taxes. They were hated by other Jews, who thought of them as traitors to their country and to their religion. ᵇ*pay back four times as much:* Both Jewish and Roman law said that a person must pay back four times the amount that was taken. ᶜ*saved:* Zacchaeus was Jewish, but it is only now that he is rescued from sin and placed under God's care. ᵈ*son of Abraham:* As used in this verse, the words mean that Zacchaeus is truly one of God's special people.

The Prodigal Son

J esus told this story to a crowd of people:

Once a man had two sons. The younger son said
to his father, "Give me my share of the property." So
the father divided his property between his two sons.

Not long after that, the younger son packed up

everything he owned and left for a foreign country, where he wasted all his money in wild living. He had spent everything, when a bad famine spread through that whole land. Soon he had nothing to eat.

He went to work for a man in that country, and the man sent him out to take care of his pigs[a]. This was a terrible job, and he was still hungry. He would have been glad to eat what the pigs were eating,[b] but no one gave him a thing.

Finally, he came to his senses and said, "My father's workers have plenty to eat, and here I am, starving to death! I will go to my father and say to him, 'Father, I have sinned against God in heaven and against you. I am no longer good enough to be called your son. Treat me like one of your workers.' "

The younger son got up and started back home to his father. But when he was still a long way off, his father saw him and felt sorry for him. He ran to his son and hugged and kissed him.

The son said, "Father, I have sinned against God in heaven and against you. I am no longer good enough to be called your son."

But his father said to the servants, "Hurry and bring the best clothes and put them on him. Give him a ring for his finger and sandals[c] for his feet. Get the best calf and prepare it, so we can eat and celebrate. This son of mine was dead, but has now come back to life. He was lost and has now been found." And they began to celebrate.

The older son had been out in the field. But when he came near the house, he heard the music and dancing. So he called one of the servants over and asked, "What's going on here?"

The servant answered, "Your brother has come home safe and sound, and your father ordered us to kill the best calf." The older brother got so angry that he would not even go into the house.

His father came out and begged him to go in. But he said to his father, "For years I have worked for you like a slave and have always obeyed you. But you have never even given me a little goat, so that I could give a dinner for my friends. This other son of yours wasted your money on foolish things. And now that he has come home, you ordered the best calf to be killed for a feast."

His father replied, "My son, you are always with me, and everything I have is yours. But we should be glad and celebrate! Your brother was dead, but he is now alive. He was lost and has now been found."

In this way, Jesus reminds us that God always loves us, even when we disobey him and try to run away from him. He continues to care for us, and when we return to him, he celebrates.

Luke 15.11–32

apigs: The Jewish religion taught that pigs were not fit to eat or even to touch. A Jewish man would have felt terribly insulted if he had to feed pigs, much less eat with them. bwhat the pigs were eating: The Greek text has "(bean) pods," which came from a tree in Palestine. These were used to feed animals. Poor people sometimes ate them, too. cring . . . sandals: These show that the young man's father fully accepted him as his son. A ring was a sign of high position in the family. Sandals showed that he was a son instead of a slave, since slaves did not usually wear sandals.

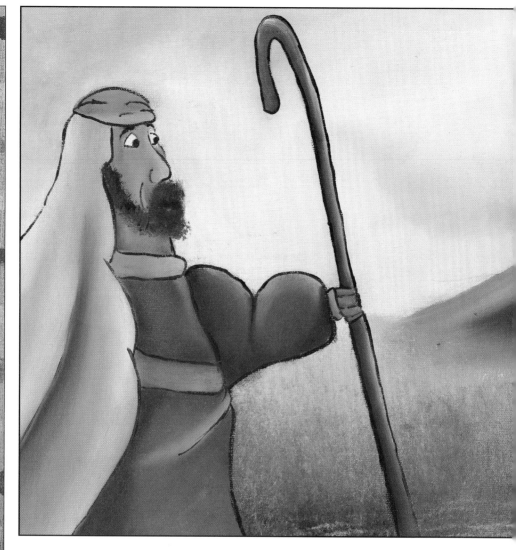

The Good Shepherd

Jesus said:

> I am the good shepherd, and the good shepherd gives up his life for his sheep. Hired workers are not like the shepherd. They don't own the sheep, and when

they see a wolf coming, they run off and leave the sheep. Then the wolf attacks and scatters the flock. Hired workers run away because they don't care about the sheep.

I am the good shepherd. I know my sheep, and they know me. Just as the Father knows me, I know the Father, and I give up my life for my sheep. I have other sheep that are not in this sheep pen. I must bring them together too, when they hear my voice. Then there will be one flock of sheep and one shepherd.

We must remember that God takes care of us, no matter what. This has always been true. The great king David knew this when he wrote:

> You, LORD, are my
> shepherd,
>   I will never be in
>   need.
> You let me rest in fields
> of green grass.
> You lead me to streams
> of peaceful water,
>   and you refresh my
>   life.
> You are true to your name,
> and you lead me
>   along the right paths.
> I may walk through valleys
> as dark as death,
>   but I won't be afraid.
> You are with me,
> and your shepherd's rod[a]
>   makes me feel safe.
> You treat me to a feast,
>   while my enemies watch.
> You honor me as your guest,
> and you fill my cup
>   until it overflows.

Your kindness and love
will always be with me
      each day of my life,
and I will live forever
      in your house, L<small>ORD</small>.

Psalm 23; John 10.11–16

^a*shepherd's rod:* The Hebrew text mentions two objects carried by the shepherd: a club to defend against wild animals and a long pole to guide and control the sheep.

The Triumphant Entry

When Jesus and his disciples came near Jerusalem, he went to Bethphage on the Mount of Olives and sent two of the disciples on ahead. He told them, "Go into the next village, where you will at once find a donkey and her colt. Untie

194

the two donkeys and bring them to me. If anyone asks why you are doing that, just say, 'The Lord[a] needs them.' Right away he will let you have the donkeys."

So God's promise came true, just as the prophet had said,

> "Announce to the people of Jerusalem:
> 'Your king is coming to you!
> He is humble and rides on a donkey.
> He comes on the colt of a donkey.' "

The disciples went off and found everything just as Jesus had said. While they were untying the donkey, the owners asked, "Why are you doing that?"

They answered, "The Lord[b] needs it."

They brought the donkey and its colt and laid some clothes on their backs. Then Jesus got on.

Many people came to honor Jesus and to welcome him into Jerusalem. They spread clothes in the road, while others put down branches[c] which they had cut from trees. Some people walked ahead of Jesus and others followed behind. They were all shouting,

"Hooray[d] for the Son of David![e]

God bless the one who comes in the name of the Lord.

Hooray for God in heaven above!"

When Jesus came to Jerusalem, everyone in the city was excited and asked, "Who can this be?"

The crowd answered, "This is Jesus, the prophet from Nazareth in Galilee."

Some Pharisees in the crowd said to Jesus, "Teacher, make your disciples stop shouting!"

But Jesus answered, "If they keep quiet, these stones will start shouting."

Once Jesus got into the city, he went to the temple to worship. But he was very angry about what he found there.

When Jesus entered the temple, he started chasing out the

people who were selling things. He told them, "The Scriptures say, 'My house should be a place of worship.' But you have made it a place where robbers hide!"

Each day, Jesus kept on teaching in the temple. So the chief priests, the teachers of the Law of Moses, and some other important people tried to have him killed. But they could not find a way to do it, because everyone else was eager to listen to him.

Matthew 21.1–5, 7–11; Luke 19.32–34, 39, 40, 45–48

aThe Lord: Or "The master of the donkeys." bThe Lord: Or "The master of the donkeys." cspread clothes . . . put down branches: This was one way that the Jewish people welcomed a famous person. dHooray: This translates a word that can mean "please save us." But it is most often used as a shout of praise to God. eSon of David: The Jewish people expected the Messiah to be from the family of King David, and for this reason the Messiah was often called the "Son of David."

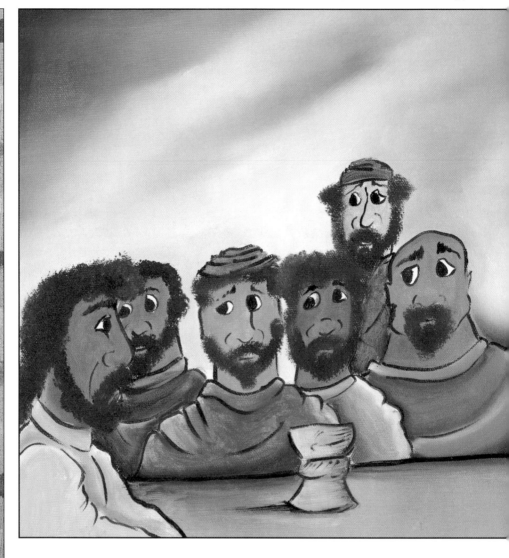

The Last Supper

On the first day of the Festival of Thin Bread, Jesus' disciples came to him and asked, "Where do you want us to prepare the Passover meal?"

Jesus told them to go to a certain man in the city and

tell him, "Our teacher says, 'My time has come! I want to eat the Passover meal with my disciples in your home.' " They did as Jesus told them and prepared the meal.

When Jesus was eating with his twelve disciples that evening, he said, "One of you will surely hand me over to my enemies."

The disciples were very sad, and each one said to Jesus, "Lord, you can't mean me!"

He answered, "One of you men who has eaten with me   *199*

from this dish will betray me. The Son of Man will die, as the Scriptures say. But it's going to be terrible for the one who betrays me! That man would be better off if he had never been born."

Judas said, "Teacher, you surely don't mean me!"

"That's what you say!" Jesus replied. But later, Judas did betray him.

During the meal Jesus took some bread in his hands. He blessed the bread and broke it. Then he gave it to his disciples and said, "Take this and eat it. This is my body."

Jesus picked up a cup of wine and gave thanks to God. He then gave it to his disciples and said, "Take this and drink it. This is my blood, and with it God makes his agreement with you. It will be poured out, so that many people will have their sins forgiven. From now on I am not going to drink any wine, until I drink new wine with you in my Father's kingdom." Then they sang a hymn and went out to the Mount of Olives.

Jesus said to his disciples, "During this very night, all of you will reject me, as the Scriptures say,

'I will strike down the shepherd,
        and the sheep will be scattered.'

But after I am raised to life, I will go to Galilee ahead of

you."

Peter spoke up, "Even if all the others reject you, I never will!"

Jesus replied, "I promise you that before a rooster crows tonight, you will say three times that you don't know me." But Peter said, "Even if I have to die with you, I will never say I don't know you."

All the others said the same thing.

Matthew 26.17–35

The Garden of Gethsemane

Jesus went with his disciples to a place called Gethsemane. When they got there, he told them, "Sit here while I go over there and pray."

Jesus took along Peter and the two brothers, James and

John.[a] He was very sad and troubled, and he said to them, "I am so sad that I feel as if I am dying. Stay here and keep awake with me."

Jesus walked on a little way. Then he knelt with his face to the ground and prayed, "My Father, if it is possible, don't make me suffer by having me drink from this cup.[b] Is there any other way I can go through this? But do what you want, and not what I want."

He came back and found his disciples sleeping. So he

said to Peter, "Can't any of you stay awake with me for just one hour? Stay awake and pray that you won't be tested. You want to do what is right, but you are weak."

Again Jesus went to pray and said, "My Father, if there is no other way, and I must suffer, I will still do what you want."

Jesus came back and found them sleeping again. They simply could not keep their eyes open. He left them and prayed the same prayer once more.

God was not forcing Jesus to do anything. Although Jesus knew that what he was about to face would be difficult, he chose to do God's will all on his own. At that moment the Lord sent an angel from heaven to give Jesus the strength that he would need to get through this very difficult time.

Finally, Jesus returned to his disciples and said, "Are you still sleeping and resting?[c] The time has come for the Son of Man to be handed over to sinners. Get up! Let's go. The one who will betray me is already here."

Jesus was still speaking, when Judas the betrayer came up. He was one of the twelve disciples, and a large mob armed with swords and clubs was with him. They had been sent by the chief priests and the nation's leaders. Judas had told them ahead of time, "Arrest the man I greet with a kiss."[d]

Judas walked right up to Jesus and said, "Hello, teacher." Then Judas kissed him.

Jesus replied, "My friend, why are you here?"[e]

The men grabbed Jesus and arrested him. One of Jesus' followers pulled out a sword. He struck the servant of the high priest and cut off his ear.

But Jesus told him, "Put your sword away. Anyone who lives by fighting will die by fighting. Don't you know that I could ask my Father, and right away he would send me more than twelve armies of angels? But then, how could the words of the Scriptures come true, which say that this must happen?"

Jesus said to the mob, "Why do you come with swords and clubs to arrest me like a criminal? Day after day I sat and taught in the temple, and you didn't arrest me. But all this happened, so that what the prophets wrote would come true."

All of Jesus' disciples left him and ran away.

Matthew 26.36–56

---

[a]*the two brothers, James and John:* The Greek text has "the two sons of Zebedee." [b]*having me drink from this cup:* In the Scriptures "to drink from a cup" sometimes means to suffer. [c]*Are you still sleeping and resting?:* Or "You may as well keep on sleeping and resting." [d]*the man I greet with a kiss:* It was the custom for people to greet each other with a kiss on the cheek. [e]*why are you here?:* Or "do what you came for."

The Road
to the Cross

After his arrest, Jesus was brought before Pilate, who was the governor. The people who had brought Jesus started accusing him and said, "We caught this man trying to get our

people to riot and to stop paying taxes to the Emperor. He also claims that he is the Messiah, our king."

Pilate asked Jesus, "Are you the king of the Jews?"

"Those are your words," Jesus answered.

Pilate told the chief priests and the crowd, "I don't find him guilty of anything."

He told them, "You brought Jesus to me and said he was a troublemaker. But I have questioned him here in front of you, and I have not found him guilty of anything that you say he has done. This man doesn't deserve to be put to death! I will just have him beaten with a whip and set free."[a]

But the whole crowd shouted, "Kill Jesus!"

Pilate wanted to set Jesus free, so he spoke again to the crowds. Pilate asked them, "Do you want me to free the king of the Jews?" Pilate knew that the chief priests had brought Jesus to him because they were jealous. Pilate obviously thought Jesus was innocent. Because there was a tradition of releasing one prisoner during Passover, Pilate was offering the people who  were accusing Jesus a way to let him go without losing their honor.

But they kept shouting, "Nail him to a cross! Nail him to a cross!"

Pilate spoke to them a third time, "But what crime has he done? I have not found him guilty of anything for which he should be put to death."

The people kept on shouting as loud as they could for Jesus to be put to death. Finally, Pilate gave in. Pilate handed Jesus over for them to do what they wanted with him.

As Jesus was being led away, some soldiers grabbed hold of Simon, a man from Cyrene, which is northern Africa. He was coming in from the fields, but they put the cross on him and made him carry it behind Jesus. Because Jesus had been beaten, he was no longer able to carry the cross.

A large crowd was following Jesus, and in the crowd a lot of women were crying and weeping for him. Jesus turned to the women and said:

Women of Jerusalem, don't cry for me! Cry for yourselves and for your children.

Mark 15.9, 10; Luke 23.1–4, 14–18a, 20–28

---

[a]*set free:* Some manuscripts add, "Pilate said this, because at every Passover he was supposed to set one prisoner free for the Jewish people."

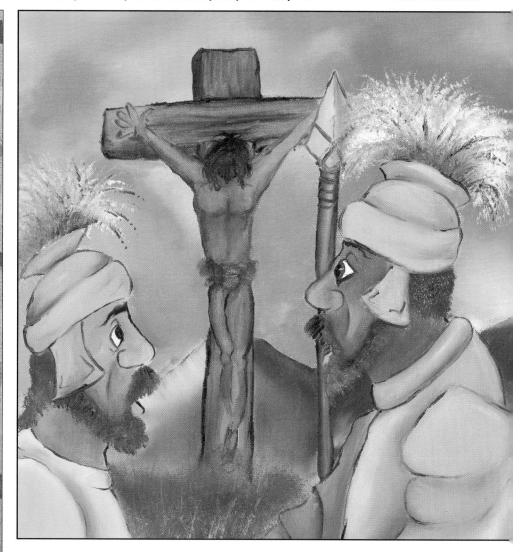

The Crucifixion

A fter Jesus had been brought before Pilate and beaten, soldiers took him to Golgotha, which means "Place of a Skull."ᵃ There they gave him some wine mixed with a drug to ease the pain, but he refused to drink it.

They nailed Jesus to a cross and gambled to see who would get his clothes. It was about nine o'clock in the morning when they nailed him to the cross. On it was a sign that told why he was nailed there. It read, "This is the King of the Jews." The soldiers also nailed two criminals on crosses, one to the right of Jesus and the other to his left.[b]

Jesus said, "Father, forgive these people! They don't know what they're doing."[c]

People who passed by said terrible things about Jesus. *211*

They shook their heads and shouted, "Ha! So you're the one who claimed you could tear down the temple and build it again in three days. Save yourself and come down from the cross!"

One of the criminals hanging there also insulted Jesus by saying, "Aren't you the Messiah? Save yourself and save us!"

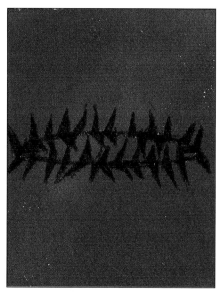

But the other criminal told the first one off, "Don't you fear God? Aren't you getting the same punishment as this man? We got what was coming to us, but he didn't do anything wrong." Then he said to Jesus, "Remember me when you come into power!"

Jesus replied, "I promise that today you will be with me in paradise."[d]

Around noon the sky turned dark and stayed that way until the middle of the afternoon. The sun stopped shining. Jesus shouted, "Father, I put myself in your hands!" Then he died.

Some women were looking on at the terrible sight. They had come with Jesus to Jerusalem. But even before this they had been his followers and had helped him. Mary Magdalene and Mary the mother of the younger James and of Joseph were two of these women. Salome was also one of them.

All of Jesus' close friends and the women who had

come with him from Galilee stood at a distance and watched.

It was now the evening before the Sabbath, and the Jewish people were getting ready for that sacred day. A man named Joseph from Arimathea was brave enough to ask Pilate for the body of Jesus. Joseph was a highly respected member of the Jewish council, and he was also waiting for God's kingdom to come.

Pilate was surprised to hear that Jesus was already dead, and he called in the army officer to find out if Jesus had been dead very long. After the officer told him, Pilate let Joseph have Jesus' body.

Joseph bought a linen cloth and took the body down from the cross. He had it wrapped in the cloth, and he put it in a tomb that had been cut into solid rock. Then he rolled a big stone against the entrance to the tomb.

Mary Magdalene and Mary the mother of Joseph were watching and saw where the body was placed.

Mark 15.22–30, 40–47; Luke 23.34, 35, 39–46, 49

---

[a]*Place of a Skull:* The place was probably given this name because it was near a large rock in the shape of a human skull. [b]*left:* Some manuscripts add, "So the Scriptures came true which say, 'He was accused of being a criminal.' " [c]*Jesus said, "Father, forgive these people! They don't know what they're doing.":* These words are not in some manuscripts. [d]*paradise:* In the Greek translation of the Old Testament, this word is used for the Garden of Eden. In New Testament times it was sometimes used for the place where God's people are happy and at rest, as they wait for the final judgment.

The Resurrection

The Sabbath was over, and it was almost daybreak on Sunday when Mary Magdalene and the other Mary went to see the tomb. Suddenly a strong earthquake struck, and the Lord's angel came down from heaven. He rolled away the

stone and sat on it. The angel looked as bright as lightning,

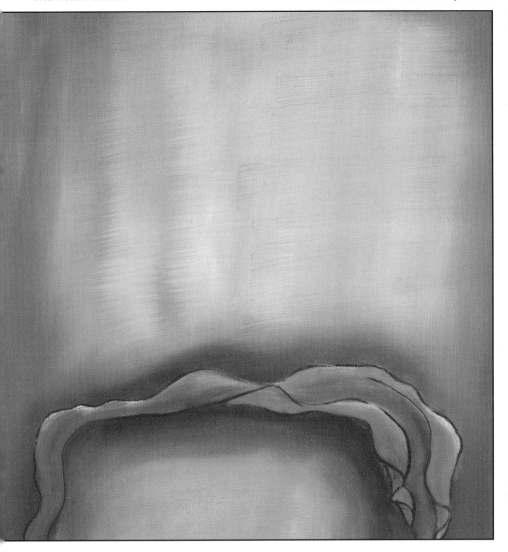

and his clothes were white as snow. The guards shook from fear and fell down, as though they were dead.

The angel said to the women, "Don't be afraid! I know you are looking for Jesus, who was nailed to a cross. He isn't here! God has raised him to life, just as Jesus said he would. Come, see the place where his body was lying. Now hurry! Tell his disciples that he has been raised to life and is on his way to Galilee. Go there, and you will see him. That is what I came to tell you."

The women were frightened and yet very happy, as they hurried from the tomb and ran to tell the disciples. Suddenly Jesus met them and greeted them. They went near him, held on to his feet, and worshiped him. Then Jesus said, "Don't be afraid! Tell my followers to go to Galilee. They will see me there."

While the women were on their way, some soldiers who had been guarding the tomb went into the city. They told the chief priests everything that had happened. So the chief priests met with the leaders and decided to bribe the soldiers with a lot of money.

They said to the soldiers, "Tell everyone that Jesus' disciples came during the night and stole his body while you were asleep. If the governor[a] hears about this, we will talk to him. You won't have anything to worry about."

The soldiers took the money and did what they were told. The people of Judea still tell each other this story.

Jesus' eleven disciples went to a mountain in Galilee, where Jesus had told them to meet him. They saw him and worshiped him, but some of them doubted.

Jesus came to them and said:

I have been given all authority in heaven and on earth! Go to the people of all nations and make them my disciples. Baptize them in the name of the Father, the Son, and the Holy Spirit, and teach them to do everything I have told you. I will be with you always, even until the end of the world.

After the Lord Jesus had said these things to the disciples, he was taken back up to heaven where he sat down at the right side[b] of God.

Matthew 28.1–20; Mark 16.19

On the Road to Emmaus

On the road to Emmaus, two of Jesus' disciples were talking and thinking about the reports that Jesus had been seen after he was crucified and buried. Just then, Jesus approached and began walking alongside of them, but they did not recognize him.

Jesus asked them, "What were you talking about as you walked along?"

The two of them stood there looking sad and gloomy. Then the one named Cleopas asked Jesus, "Are you the only person from Jerusalem who didn't know what was happening there these last few days?"

"What do you mean?" Jesus asked.

They answered:

    Those things that happened to Jesus from

Nazareth. By what he did and said he showed that he was a powerful prophet, who pleased God and all the people. Then the chief priests and our leaders had him arrested and sentenced to die on a cross. We had hoped that he would be the one to set Israel free! But it has already been three days since all this happened.

Some women in our group surprised us. They had gone to the tomb early in the morning, but did not find the body of Jesus. They came back, saying that they had seen a vision of angels who told them that he is alive. Some men from our group went to the tomb and found it just as the women had said. But they didn't see Jesus either.

Then Jesus asked the two disciples, "Why can't you understand? How can you be so slow to believe all that the prophets said? Didn't you know that the Messiah would have to suffer before he was given his glory?" Jesus then explained everything written about himself in the Scriptures.

When the two of them came near the village where they were going, Jesus seemed to be going farther. They begged him, "Stay with us! It's already late, and the sun is going down." So Jesus went into the house to stay with them.

After Jesus sat down to eat, he took some bread. He blessed it and broke it. Then he gave it to them. At once they knew who he was, but he disappeared. They said to each other, "When he talked with us along the road and explained the Scriptures to us, didn't it warm our hearts?" So they got right up and returned to Jerusalem.

The two disciples found the eleven apostles and the others gathered together. And they learned from the group that the Lord was really alive and had appeared to Peter. Then the disciples from Emmaus told what happened on the road and how they knew he was the Lord when he broke the bread.

Luke 24.13–35

Doubting Thomas

On the same day that he appeared to Mary outside his tomb, Jesus appeared that evening to all the disciples.

The disciples were afraid of the Jewish leaders, and on the evening of that same Sunday they had locked themselves in a room. Suddenly, Jesus appeared in the middle of the

group. He greeted them and showed them his hands and his side—his wounds from being nailed to the cross. When the disciples saw the Lord, they became very happy.

After Jesus had greeted them, he said, "I am sending you, just as the Father has sent me." Then he breathed on them and said, "Receive the Holy Spirit. If you forgive anyone's sins, they will be forgiven. But if you don't forgive their sins, they will not be forgiven."

Although Thomas the Twin was one of the twelve　*223*

disciples, he wasn't with the others when Jesus appeared to them. So they told him, "We have seen the Lord!"

But Thomas refused to believe. He said, "First, I must see the nail scars in his hands and touch them with my finger. I must put my hand where the spear went into his side. I won't believe unless I do this!" Thomas was full of doubt.

A week later the disciples were together again. This time, Thomas was with them. Jesus came in while all the doors were still locked and stood in the middle of the group. He greeted his disciples and said to Thomas, "Put your finger here and look at my hands! Put your hand into my side. Stop doubting and have faith!"

Thomas replied, "You are my Lord and my God!"

Jesus said, "Thomas, do you have faith because you have seen me? The people who have faith in me without seeing me are the ones who are really blessed!"

Jesus later appeared to his disciples along the shore of Lake Tiberias. Simon Peter, Thomas the Twin, Nathanael from Cana in Galilee, and the brothers James and John,[a] were there, together with two other disciples. Simon Peter said, "I'm going fishing!"

The others said, "We will go with you." They went out in their boat. But they didn't catch a thing that night.

Early the next morning Jesus stood on the shore, but

the disciples did not realize who he was. Jesus shouted, "Friends, have you caught anything?"

"No!" they answered.

So he told them, "Let your net down on the right side of your boat, and you will catch some fish."

They did, and the net was so full of fish that they could not drag it up into the boat.

When the disciples got out of the boat, they saw some bread and a charcoal fire with fish on it. Jesus told his disciples, "Bring some of the fish you just caught."

Jesus said, "Come and eat!" But none of the disciples dared ask who he was. They knew he was the Lord. Jesus took the bread in his hands and gave some of it to his disciples. He did the same with the fish. This was the third time that Jesus appeared to his disciples after he was raised from death.

Jesus worked many other miracles for his disciples, and not all of them are written in this book. The miracles that are recorded in the Bible are so that you will put your faith in Jesus as the Messiah and the Son of God. If you have faith in him, you will have true life.

John 20.19–31; 21.1–6, 9, 10, 12–14

Peter and John on Trial

After Jesus came and spoke to the disciples and filled them with the Holy Spirit, the disciples went out and performed miracles in the name of Jesus. Peter and John healed a man who could not walk. Teaching the people God's law angered the priests and other officials. So they had Peter and

John arrested. Already a lot of people had heard the disciples' message and believed it.

The leaders, the elders, and teachers of the Law of Moses met in Jerusalem. They brought in Peter and John and made them stand in the middle while they questioned them. They asked, "By what power and in whose name have you done this?"

Peter was filled with the Holy Spirit and told the nation's leaders and the elders:

You are questioning us today about a kind deed in which a crippled man was healed. But there is something we must tell you and everyone else in Israel. This man is standing here completely well because of

the power of Jesus Christ from Nazareth. You put Jesus to death on a cross, but God raised him to life. Only Jesus has the power to save! His name is the only one in all the world that can save anyone.

The officials were amazed to see how brave Peter and John were, and they knew that these two apostles were only ordinary men and not well educated. The officials were certain that these men had been with Jesus. But they could not deny what had happened. The man who had been healed was standing there with the apostles.

The officials commanded them to leave the council room. Then the officials said to each other, "What can we do with these men? Everyone in Jerusalem knows about this miracle, and we cannot say it didn't happen. But to keep this thing from spreading, we will warn them never again to speak to anyone about the name of Jesus." So they called the two apostles back in and told them that they must never, for any reason, teach anything about the name of Jesus.

Peter and John answered, "Do you think God wants us

to obey you or to obey him? We cannot keep quiet about what we have seen and heard."

The officials could not find any reason to punish Peter and John. So they threatened them and let them go. The man who was healed by this miracle was more than forty years old, and everyone was praising God for what had happened.

Acts 4.5, 7–10, 12–22

Saul on the Road to Damascus

There were many who hated Jesus. Saul was an evil man who especially hated Jesus and all his followers. At that time the church in Jerusalem suffered terribly. All of the Lord's followers, except the apostles, were scattered every-

where in Judea and Samaria. Saul started making a lot of trouble for the church. He went from house to house arresting men and women and putting them in jail.

Saul kept on threatening to kill the Lord's followers. He even went to the high priest and asked for letters to their leaders in Damascus. He did this because he wanted to arrest and take to Jerusalem any man or woman who had accepted the Lord's Way. When Saul had almost reached Damascus, a bright light from heaven suddenly flashed around him. He fell to the ground and heard a voice that said, "Saul! Saul! Why are you so cruel to me?"

"Who are you?" Saul asked.

"I am Jesus," the Lord answered. "I am the one you are so cruel to. Now get up and go into the city, where you will be told what to do."

The men with Saul stood there speechless. They had heard the voice, but they had not seen anyone. Saul got up from the ground, and when he opened his eyes, he could not see a thing. Someone then led him by the hand to Damascus, and for three days he was blind and did not eat or drink.

A follower named Ananias lived in Damascus, and the Lord spoke to him in a vision. Ananias answered, "Lord, here I am."

The Lord said to him, "Get up and go to the house of Judas on Straight Street. When you get there, you will find a man named Saul from the city of Tarsus. Saul is praying, and he has seen a vision. He saw a man named Ananias coming to him and putting his hands on him, so that he could see again."

Ananias replied, "Lord, a lot of people have told me about the terrible things this man has done to your followers in Jerusalem. Now the chief priests have given him the power to come here and arrest anyone who worships in your name."

The Lord said to Ananias, "Go! I have chosen him to

tell foreigners, kings, and the people of Israel about him. I will show him how much he must suffer for worshiping in my name."

Ananias left and went into the house where Saul was staying. Ananias placed his hands on him and said, "Saul, the Lord Jesus has sent me. He is the same one who appeared to you along the road. He wants you to be able to see and to be filled with the Holy Spirit."

Suddenly something like fish scales fell from Saul's eyes, and he could see. He got up and was baptized. Then he ate and felt much better.

For several days Saul stayed with the Lord's followers in Damascus. Soon he went to the Jewish meeting places and started telling people that Jesus is the Son of God. Everyone who heard Saul was amazed because they remembered the old Saul. Saul became a great speaker for the Lord.

Acts 8.1–3; 9.1–22

Philip
and the Ethiopian

Jerusalem had been the main place that the gospel had been preached, until the Lord's followers were run out of town by the enemies of Jesus. Perhaps they thought they would stop the spread of the gospel, but this was not the case.

In fact, the opposite happened and fulfilled what Jesus said his followers should do: Take the gospel to all nations.

The Lord's followers who had been scattered went from place to place, telling the good news.

Philip went to the city of Samaria and told the people about Christ. They crowded around Philip because they were eager to hear what he was saying and to see him work miracles.

Many people with evil spirits were healed, and the   *235* spirits went out of them with a shout. A lot of crippled and lame people were also healed. Everyone in that city was very glad because of what was happening.

After Philip had been in Samaria for some time, the Lord's angel said to him, "Go south[a] along the desert road that leads from Jerusalem to Gaza."[b] So Philip left.

An important Ethiopian official happened to be going along that road in his chariot. He was the chief treasurer for Candace, the Queen of Ethiopia, and a very important man. The official had gone to Jerusalem to worship and was now on his way home. He was sitting in his chariot, reading the book of the prophet Isaiah.

The Spirit told Philip to catch up with the chariot. Philip ran up close and heard the man reading aloud from the book of Isaiah. Philip asked him, "Do you understand what you are reading?"

The Ethiopian official answered, "How can I understand unless someone helps me?" He then invited Philip to come up and sit beside him.

The official said to Philip, "Tell me, what was the prophet talking about?" So Philip began at this place in the Scriptures and explained the good news about Jesus.

As they were going along the road, they came to a place where there was some water. The official said, "Look! Here is some water. Why can't I be baptized?"ᶜ He ordered the chariot to stop. Then they both went down into the water, and Philip baptized him.

After they came out of the water, the Lord's Spirit took Philip away. The official never saw him again, but he was very happy as he went on his way.

Acts 8.25–31, 34–39

ᵃ*Go south:* Or "About noon go." ᵇ*the desert road that leads from Jerusalem to Gaza:* Or "The road that leads from Jerusalem to Gaza in the desert." ᶜ*"Why can't I be baptized:* Some manuscripts add, "Philip replied, 'You can, if you believe with all your heart.' The official answered, 'I believe that Jesus Christ is the Son of God.'"

Paul's Journeys

Jesus commanded his disciples, "You will tell everyone about me in Jerusalem, in all Judea, in Samaria, and everywhere in the world." He wanted everyone to hear the message of salvation. Paul was a disciple of Jesus Christ and spread the gospel to more people outside the Jewish faith than anyone else.

Paul made three journeys to spread the good news of Jesus Christ. On one of the trips, Paul and Silas were thrown into jail for sending an evil spirit out of a slave girl.

About midnight Paul and Silas were praying and singing praises to God, while the other prisoners listened. Suddenly a strong earthquake shook the jail to its foundations. The doors opened, and the chains fell from all the prisoners. When the jailer woke up and saw that the doors were open, he thought that the prisoners had escaped. He pulled out his sword and was about to kill himself. But Paul shouted, "Don't harm yourself! No one has escaped."

The jailer asked for a torch and went into the jail. He was shaking all over as he knelt down in front of Paul and Silas. After he had led them out of jail, he asked, "What must I do to be saved?"

They replied, "Have faith in the Lord Jesus and you will be saved! This is also true for everyone who lives in your home."

On another trip, Paul is again a prisoner being transported by boat to Rome to be tried by the Emperor. On the way, the ship was caught in a terrible storm. The storm was so fierce that they threw some of the ship's cargo overboard, trying to keep the ship from sinking. For several days they could not see either the sun or the stars. A strong wind kept blowing, and they finally gave up all hope of being saved.

But Paul stood up and told the men, "I belong to God, and I worship him. God will save the lives of everyone on the ship. But we will first be shipwrecked on some island."

For fourteen days and nights, the ship was blown around. Finally, the ship's crew saw a coast with a beach. They ran the ship aground. The captain ordered everyone who could swim to dive into the water and head for shore. Then he told the others to hold on to planks of wood or parts

of the ship. At last, everyone safely reached shore.

This island was called Malta, and the people who lived there welcomed the crew. Paul healed the father of the governor. Everyone on the island brought their sick people to Paul, and they were all healed. The people were very respectful to the sailors, and, when they finally sailed, they gave them everything they needed.

Acts 1.8; 16.16–31; 27.18–21,
23a, 24b, 26, 39, 44; 28.1, 2, 4–10

Timothy

Timothy was one of the greatest students of the apostle Paul. Although Timothy was the son of a Greek father and a Jewish Christian mother, he traveled many miles with Paul, who loved him as if he were Paul's own son.

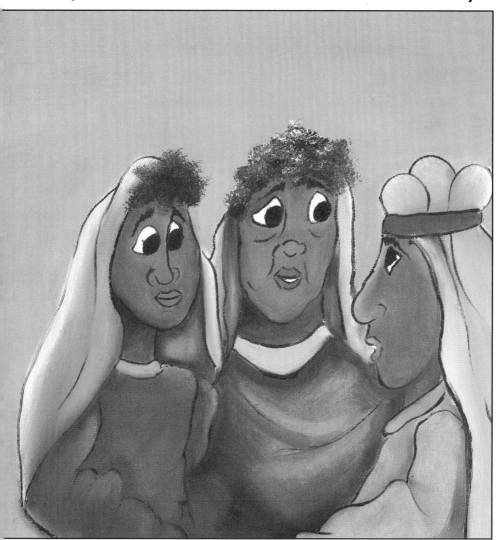

When they were not traveling together, Paul often wrote to his student to give him instructions on how to live and how to teach the good news about Jesus. Paul knew that he was not the only one who had taught Timothy.

Timothy had learned much about the Scriptures from his Christian mother and grandmother. Timothy had learned so much from them that he was truly ready for Paul's teaching. Timothy was the one responsible for strengthening the church in Macedonia, and Paul sent him on many missions to Thessalonia and Corinth.

Timothy was young, and Paul tried to guide and teach him to be a better servant of the Lord. Timothy was sensitive, affectionate, and loyal, but he still suffered from temptations and fearfulness.

Paul's second letter to Timothy reminds us of how much Paul loved God and wanted to show Timothy and all of those who love Jesus how to live the way Jesus wants us to.

Paul wrote:

Timothy, you are like a dear child to me. I pray that God our Father and our Jesus Christ Jesus will be kind and merciful to you and will bless you with peace!

Night and day I mention you in my prayers. I am always grateful for you, as I pray to the God my ancestors and I have served with a clear conscience. I remember how you cried, and I want to see you, because that will make me truly happy. I also remember the genuine faith of your mother Eunice. Your grandmother Lois had the same sort of faith, and I am sure that you have it as well. So I ask you to make full use of the gift that God gave you. Use it well. God's Spirit[a] doesn't make cowards out of us. The Spirit gives

us power, love, and self-control.

Don't be ashamed to speak for our Lord. Use the power that comes from God and join with me in suffering for telling the good news.

Christ our Savior defeated death
　　　and brought us the good news.
It shines like a light and offers life that never ends.

2 Timothy 1.2–8, 10